To Andrew,
with best wishes
Paul Salveson

Moorlands, Memories and Reflections

A centenary celebration of Allen Clarke's
Moorlands and Memories

Paul Salveson

2020

Moorlands, Memories and Reflections

A centenary celebration of Allen Clarke's
Moorlands and Memories

109 Harpers Lane, Bolton BL1 6HU
www.lancashireloominary.co.uk

ISBN 978-0-9559171-7-2

Lancashire Loominary

November 2020

Acknowledgments

Many thanks to everyone who has helped me with this book.

As always, and despite the restrictions imposed by the Covid-19 Lockdown, the support from Bolton Library and Museum Services has been tremendous. Halliwell Local History Society, Horwich Heritage and Turton Local History Society have all been enormously helpful. In no particular order, many thanks to Andrew Rosthorn, Stuart Whittle, Andy Martindale, Andrew Bibby, Jean Seymour, Harold Heys, Vernon Sidlow, Steve Leyland, Rob Gamble (DC Graphics), Linda Nuttall and the staff of Minerva Press. And a huge thanks to Maxine Peake for her foreword.

All photographs are by the author unless credited otherwise.

Printed by Minerva Press, Bolton. Design by DC Graphics, York

Allen Clarke

An invitation from Allen Clarke

"Though the town in its development and extension has encroached more and more upon the moorlands, there are still plenty left, enough and more than enough, for joyous and healthy rambles, rides, excursions, explorations – botanical, geological, historical, antiquarian, or merely recreational. So come with me, and starting from Bolton-le-Moors, have a look at Lancashire's moorlands."

Allen Clarke, *Moorlands and Memories*, 1920

Contents

Foreword

Maxine Peake

Maxine Peake

Hill walking, cycling, literature, philosophy, protest and The North.... 'These are a few of my favourite things'. Paul Salveson's new book on Allen Clarke is irresistible. I might even be as bold to say Paul is the Allen Clarke for our times, charting northern working class radical history and the rural landscape that has influenced and been a constant backdrop to the struggle for a better world.

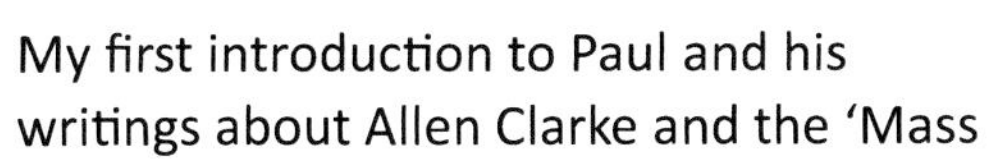

My first introduction to Paul and his writings about Allen Clarke and the 'Mass Trespass' movement was his 1982 publication *Will Yo' Come O' Sunday Mornin' - The 1896 Battle For Winter Hill*. Admittedly I was just eight years old then so it wasn't on my reading list at the time, but resided on a book shelf at my Step Grandfather's, Jim Taylor. I had though, that same year, been taken on the march over Winter Hill to commemorate the trespass.

Jim lived on Old Lords Estate in Horwich, so weekends with Jim and my Nan, Ellen, were spent in the shadow of Winter Hill and Rivington Pike. I remember very vividly the fantastic atmosphere as we hiked over the moors that September day.

These were the moors I was so familiar with. I played here, I learnt to ride my bike here, spent hours skimming stones on the reservoir. Hours walking with Jim as he pointed out wildlife and taught me the names of plants, birds and trees.

As an eight-year old I found it hard contemplating that this was a right that had to be fought for. That September day was a mass gathering of liked-minded comrades celebrating and remembering a significant event in Lancashire's history. It was also a stark reminder that the battle against land ownership was not over.

I didn't become interested in politics until a few years later but I will never forget being taught that day about the strong connection between the countryside and how all our freedoms depend on our 'right to roam'. As Paul shows throughout this book, love of our Lancashire countryside has always been at the heart of progressive working class politics.

Introduction: Allen Clarke's *Moorlands and Memories*

"..we will chat of the things we see on the road, bits of history, romance, folk-lore, in short, anything that may crop up, ancient or modern, characters dead and gone, living folk we meet on walks and rides, for sometimes we shall be afoot, while at others we shall utilise that condenser of distance, the helpful wheel that halves the miles – the bicycle."[1]

This book is a celebration of Allen Clarke's Lancashire classic, *Moorlands and Memories*, published a hundred years ago. He wrote in an easy, conversational style - unusual for its time. I hope that this tribute to his masterpiece is as relaxed, meandering and informal as his own book.

Allen Clarke was one of Lancashire's greatest writers but is virtually forgotten today. He was born in Bolton in 1863, at 58 Parrot Street Daubhill, the son of mill workers. He went to work in the mill himself at the age of 11 but was fortunate in having parents who encouraged his love of reading and writing. In the face of huge difficulties, he developed his own brand of popular journalism, mixing socialist politics with Lancashire dialect, humour and wisdom. [2]

He became better known by his pseudonym of 'Teddy Ashton', though he had several others. His *Tum Fowt Sketches*, featuring the anarchic doings of Bill and Bet Spriggs, became hugely popular amongst working class readers in the cotton towns of South Lancashire and the West Riding. His newspapers – notably *The Trotter* and subsequently *Teddy Ashton's Northern Weekly* - were read by tens of thousands.

Clarke was an amazingly diverse writer. Between 1896 and 1908 he managed to bring out a weekly newspaper which he mostly wrote himself. But that was only part of his work. Over 20 novels were serialised in his papers and in other publications such as *Liverpool Weekly Post* or *The Cotton Factory Times*; some later appeared in book form. He wrote poetry, short stories, social and political commentaries and philosophical essays.

He wrote extensively about the Lancashire countryside, which he explored on foot and bike. He always maintained that there were 'three Lancashires'. The

---

[1] Allen Clarke, *Moorlands and Memories*, p.4. References are to the 3rd edition (Bolton, 1924). From here, references to the book are just shown as *Moorlands*

[2] See Paul Salveson *Lancashire's Romantic Radical: The Life and Writings of Allen Clarke/Teddy Ashton*, Slaithwaite 2009

Lancashire of the factories, mines and mills and the softer face of the county, in what he called 'Windmill Land' stretching from Preston to Blackpool and the Fylde. But there was also a 'Moorland Lancashire' which he celebrated in *Moorlands and Memories*.

The book was first published by the newspaper company Tillotson's of Bolton in 1920. It was based mostly on a series of articles that Allen Clarke wrote in *The Bolton Journal and Guardian* in the previous couple of years.

As the title suggests, it is more than a book about 'the moorlands'. The 'memories' in the title go back to his childhood and upbringing in mid-Victorian Bolton. It is an intensely personal account, speaking of people he knew and loved. It is a truly remarkable collection of anecdote, history, literature, philosophy and fine descriptions of Lancashire scenery.

Some of the articles were written when the First World War was still raging. It was published less than two years after it had ended, leaving millions of dead and bereaved. It casts a shadow across the book, though Clarke is never despondent. His attitude towards 'the war to end all wars' is sadness and at times outrage. There is no glorification of war nor mindless jingoism.

The book introduced me to some forgotten aspects of Bolton's political and cultural history: the Winter Hill 'Trespass' of 1896 and the remarkable story of Bolton's links with Walt Whitman. I've published short histories of both – and I keep discovering more about them. I've updated the story, where I can, in here.

Moorlands and Memories went into three editions, with some minor additions and photographs in the last edition published in 1924. It wasn't until 1986 that a reprint of that 3rd edition became available to a new generation of readers.

This book then is a celebration of Clarke's book and his reflections on life and landscape, with some of my own. It includes a glance at what has happened over the last hundred years and a bit of speculation as to what Allen Clarke would have made of it all.

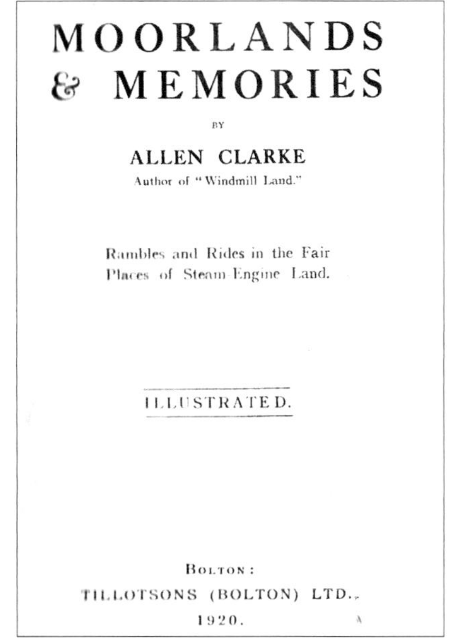
MOORLANDS
& MEMORIES

BY

ALLEN CLARKE

Author of "Windmill Land."

Rambles and Rides in the Fair Places of Steam Engine Land.

ILLUSTRATED.

BOLTON:
TILLOTSONS (BOLTON) LTD.,
1920.

Frontispiece of the 1st edition of *Moorlands and Memories*, 1920

1. Who was Allen Clarke?

"I am just as much a cyclist or scientist as I am a spiritualist or socialist" – Allen Clarke, 1903

I discovered Allen Clarke when I was a student at Lancaster University in the 1970s. Mooching about in the library I came across a collection of dialect sketches set in my home town, Bolton. They were funny, perceptive and socially incisive. The author was 'Teddy Ashton' who, it turned out, was a writer called Allen Clarke. It began a close and life-long friendship, though we have yet to meet.

Clarke, born in Bolton in 1863, became one of the North's most popular dialect writers, following in the footsteps of Edwin Waugh, Ben Brierley and Samuel Laycock, a generation later. He was at his peak between the mid-1890s and late 1920s, with thousands of devoted readers amongst the mill workers of Lancashire and Yorkshire. He was best known by his 'Teddy Ashton' pen-name which he used for his *Tum Fowt Sketches* set in 'Tum Fowt' (Tonge Fold) just outside Bolton.

Researching Clarke's life in Bolton back in the 1980s I could still find old mill workers who fondly remembered 'Teddy Ashton' and even had well-thumbed copies of his *Lancashire Annuals* - but had never heard of Allen Clarke![3]

Unit of production: Bolton spinning mill around 1900. The 'little piecer' is the lad in the background. The 'minder' is the man on the right. His 'side piecer' is on the left of the picture. *Photo courtesy of Bolton Library and Museum Services*

[3] For a fuller account of his life see *Lancashire's Romantic Radical*

The Clarke family: spinners and weavers

He was the son of cotton workers. His father emigrated from Co. Mayo in the 1840s to find work in the Lancashire mills; he was able to move up the ranks to become a 'minder', one of the aristocrats of the working class. His mother was from Warrington and worked as a weaver. It was a highly intellectual family, with a bookshelf full of 'the classics' as well as the work of dialect writers such as Sam Laycock.

The family briefly moved to Mirfield, in the West Riding, when Allen was 11, probably because his father had been blacklisted for his union activities in Bolton. He started his first job, as a 'little piecer', in a local mill. He hated it. When the family returned to Bolton a year later he started working full-time as a piecer for his father, at Gilnow Mill. The building survives but it doesn't spin any cotton.

He was able to see at first hand the realities of 'the factory system' and though he was well treated both by his father and the kindly mill manager, he hated the danger, drudgery and ill health that he and his young workmates had to endure. This experience of mill work gave him a burning sense of injustice which inspired and drove his campaign against child labour in the mills in the 1890s.

First steps as a writer

He managed to escape from factory life and after a brief time as a 'pupil teacher' at a local school and a few other jobs he took the risk of starting his own paper – *The Labour Light*. Without, as he later reminisced, *"a ha'porth of capital."* Though not a commercial success it gave him the confidence to try his hand at professional journalism. For a couple of years he published and edited *The Trotter*, a Bolton-based paper which included his dialect sketches and some of his early novels, published chapter by chapter each week. He then got a job writing for the Lancashire-based *Cotton Factory Times* and its sister *The Yorkshire Factory Times*. In 1896 he once again set up his own paper, *Teddy Ashton's Northern Weekly* (initially called *Teddy Ashton's Journal)*. This time it was a success, reaching an estimated readership of about 50,000 a week at its peak in the late 1890s.

His readership was overwhelmingly working class, as shown by the huge volume of readers' letters from weavers, 'minders' (cotton spinners), railwaymen and engineers in South Lancashire and the West Riding. As we shall see, children were avid and engaged readers. Clarke saw himself as being part of that Northern industrial working class, and wrote both serious and comic stories about ordinary people's lives in the mills, weaving sheds and mines.

Clarke wrote much of the copy for his *Northern Weekly* but encouraged other working class writers, some of whom we'll meet. His novels were about life in the Lancashire and Yorkshire industrial towns and cities, such as *The Knobstick* - set in Bolton during the 1887 Engineers' Strike.

He was a good poet and his 'Gradely Prayer' is still recited at Lancashire gatherings – though the author is often cited as that famous laureate 'Anonymous'! But perhaps his finest poetry was in the collection published as *Voices* in 1896, in particular 'The Voice of the Half-Timers', which burns with indignation against the iniquitous system of child labour:

> *"We maun moil while others play,*
> *'Mong aw th'snaky straps an' bands*
> *That snap off fingers, tangle honds,*
> *Jerk off arms by th'root an' e'en,*
> *Sometimes murder us off t'scene..."*[4]

He used his newspaper to develop a highly personal message, treating his readers as part of an extended family. His 'Editor's Gossip' was just that, sharing his ideas and experiences with his readers and inviting them to respond. The 'Children's Corner' encouraged hundreds of boys and girls, as a young as 7 or 8, to write in about 'serious' issues like child labour, as well as comment on more traditional children's pastimes. In the early 1900s, as we see later, he started his 'Teddy Ashton Picnics', the first of which attracted around 10,000 visitors to Barrow Bridge, on the outskirts of Bolton. Later picnics took place at Hardcastle Crags, Holcombe Hill, Rivington and other Northern beauty spots.

Allen Clarke's work had a radical political edge; he used comedy to attack the social evils of the time. He once wrote (of his alter ego): *"I daresay Teddy Ashton's droll sketches have done more to help reforms than far more pretentious and direct articles. For 'Teddy' even in his comic dialect sketches, pokes sly fun and undermining sarcasm at the iniquities and social injustices of the day."* [5]

A vision for a new Lancashire

He wrote 'serious' works as well, including *The Effects of the Factory System*, a searing indictment of conditions in the Lancashire mills. Tolstoy had the book translated into Russian and the two men corresponded. [6]

---

[4] From 'Voice of the Half-Timers' in C. Allen Clarke *Voices*, Manchester 1896

[5] In *Teddy Ashton's Northern Weekly*, August 26th 1905

[6] See *Lancashire's Romantic Radical*, p.48

Clarke was always on the side of the underdog and supported many unpopular causes, from women's emancipation to the ending of child labour. He was a staunch environmentalist, outraged at the damage inflicted on his beloved Lancashire by the factory system. He was strongly opposed to the Boer War and was a pacifist for most of his life.

He tried to put his ideals into practice by setting up a co-operative community near Blackpool, The Daisy Colony. But perhaps his most practical achievements were the walking and cycling events and picnics, which attracted thousands. But you could say that his greatest achievement of all was to make people laugh.

Allen Clarke and his wife Lila with their bikes outside the house that was part of 'The Daisy Colony' at Carleton, near Blackpool, about 1904

He was deeply interested in philosophy and had a fascination for eastern religious thought at a time when it was little known in the west. His book *What is Man?* is essentially a western take on classic Buddhist teaching. He became interested in spiritualism and his book *The Eternal Question* is a melding of classic Buddhism and contemporary spiritualism, which was hugely popular in the North of England before and after the First World War.

A mony-sided mon

Clarke was a great networker. He encouraged a new generation of working class writers, offering them space in his *Teddy Ashton's Northern Weekly*. They included Robert Brodie, Sam Fitton, James Haslam, Sarah Robinson, Alf Pearce, Fred Plant and many others. He brought them together in the convivial surroundings of a

Rochdale restaurant in April 1909, on the occasion of Tim Bobbin's 200th anniversary. Over tea and cakes He made the suggestion that an association of Lancashire writers might not be a bad idea. Within six months the Lancashire Authors' Association had been formed, with Clarke as its first chairman. It is still very much alive and well today.

The family moved permanently to Blackpool in the early twentieth century and Clarke became a popular local figure, establishing his own shop and a network of rambling and cycling clubs. He wrote his most popular book, *Windmill Land*, about the Fylde countryside. It's an exotic mix of local history and folklore, based around his cycling trips and rambling expeditions – a 'rustic' version of *Moorlands and Memories*.

Allen Clarke died in December 1935, walking and cycling right up to the end. It's a pity there is no memorial to him in his home town of Bolton. However, Little Marton Mill - celebrated in *Windmill Land* - has been preserved as a monument to this 'man who loved windmills', thanks to the efforts of local volunteers not least Clarke's great-grand-daughter Shirley.

His output was vast. His dialect writings are funnier than anything better-known writers such as Ben Brierley or John Hartley wrote, and his novels about working class life are infinitely more readable than Robert Tressell's *Ragged Trousered Philanthropists*. But he was also a thinker, inspired by Tolstoy, Buddhism and spiritualism. He did things, he made folk laugh; he was a do-er....a many-sided man.

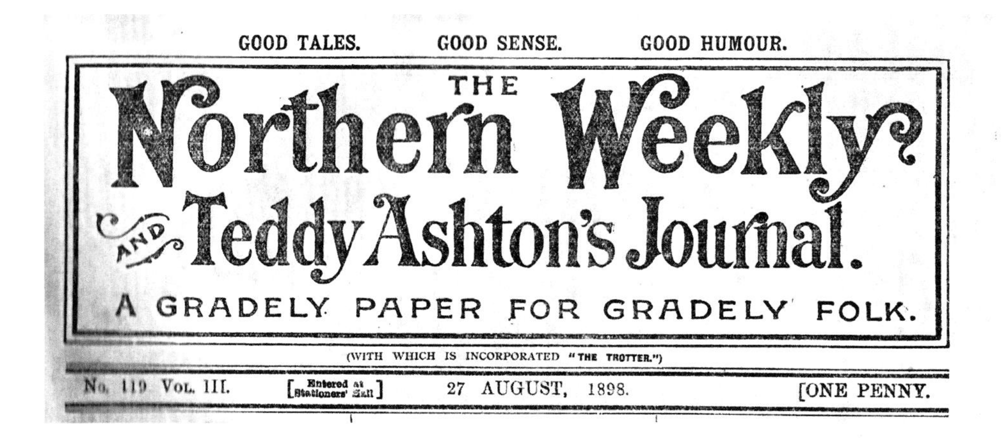
GOOD TALES. GOOD SENSE. GOOD HUMOUR.

THE Northern Weekly and Teddy Ashton's Journal.

A GRADELY PAPER FOR GRADELY FOLK.

(WITH WHICH IS INCORPORATED "THE TROTTER.")

No. 119 VOL. III. [Entered at Stationers' Hall] 27 AUGUST, 1898. [ONE PENNY.

2. A Man and his Bicycle

"I have no property, no land,
Nor gold or silver to fling,
But give me my bike and a day and a pipe,
And I have everything"[7]

Moorlands and Memories was written from the saddle of his bike. Clarke loved cycling and had a very close relationship with his bicycle. What sort of bike it was, or whether it was 'upgraded' as bicycle technology improved after the First World War, we don't know. He didn't seem particularly bothered about the technical aspect of cycling, but elevated his humble bike to an almost spiritual plane. He wrote:

"Of course you're hardly absolutely alone when out on a bicycle for a bicycle is a companion, as well as a machine to ride. Indeed I believe my bicycle is a sentient being, only a little lower than angels. It seems to share my every thought and feeling; responding with a sympathy as sweet as rare. It is a chum. It is myself extended and spread out in wheels and steel. It is a pulsing amplification of my own personality; an artificial elaboration of my own hands and feet – and may I add – heart and soul? It is a comrade."[8]

Clarke took up cycling in the late 1880s. His papers such as *Teddy Ashton's Journal*, then *Northern Weekly*, often featured adverts for cycle shops and cycle manufactures, including Tam o'Shanter cycles in Liverpool and 'The Wilcox' in Birmingham. For several years *The Northern Weekly* carried a regular cycling column, written by 'Cyclo'. It featured handy advice on buying a new machine, routine maintenance and choosing the correct saddle. Clarke was promoting cycling in his satirical newspaper *The Trotter* as early as 1892. He applauded its rapid growth from the late 1880s and proudly announced the purchase of a bicycle by his comic hero Bill Spriggs.[9]

Owd Tom

Whilst Clarke never seems very concerned with the technical aspects of cycling, he knew a chap who was – Tom Hughes. 'Owd Tom' as he became known was for

---

[7] Allen Clarke *Windmill Land*, 1916 p.285

[8] *Moorlands* p.53

[9] 'Bill Spriggs Gets a Bicycle', *The Trotter* November 25th 1892. See *Lancashire's Romantic Radical* for more on Clarke and cycling

many years a champion cyclist and ran a bike shop at 190 Wallgate, Wigan. [10] Clarke ran adverts for Tom's shop in his various publications. They were cycling companions, having met on a pilgrimage to 'Sammy Buttercup's Grave' at Croft, near Warrington, in 1904. In a postcard to a friend at the time of Clarke's death in December 1935, Tom said of that first meeting: *"we have been pals ever since."*

One obvious problem for cyclists in the 1890s was the state of the roads. This was before tarmac came into use and roads were either 'dirt' or – even worse – cobbled. When Clarke was writing in the late 1890s the pneumatic tyre was a recent innovation. But he still says, as late as 1920: *"Despite the easing tyres, though, one must admit that the roads that link the Lancashire towns are mostly a shake and a penance for the cyclist, because of the stone-paving process necessary for the heavy traffic. Yet for all that, I think them the most wondrous roads in the world."* [11]

Allen Clarke and 'Owd Tom' Hughes photographed on their way to Wembley in 1924

As well as the state of the Lancashire roads, Clarke comments at some length about particularly steep hills – the climb up Station Road into Blackrod village and the ascent up Longshaw Ford Road beyond Barrow Bridge. I wonder at what stage Clarke's bike – and that of his wife – had gears? And what would he make of the electric bike? I suspect he would have welcomed it, particularly in his later years.

---

[10] See Albert Winstanley *Owd Tom – A Cycling Legend* Wigan, 1992. Hughes had several cycling shops in the Wigan area at different times in his career.

[11] *Moorlands* p.4

The Clarion

He did much to promote cycling as an affordable and sociable form of recreation and travel. The most significant development in working class cycling activity in the 1890s was the founding of the Clarion Cycling Club in 1894 in Birmingham. It was a direct spin-off from Robert Blatchford's hugely influential *Clarion* newspaper which helped spread a distinctly Northern form of ethical socialism. Branches of the cycling club spread rapidly across the North and it was notable for its inclusivity. Women riders were welcomed alongside men, and many marriages resulted from meeting 'with the Clarion'. His serialised novel *For a Man's Sake* features a love story involving Charlie and Babs who meet through cycle outings organised by 'The Equality Church', a fictionalised amalgam of the Labour Church and Clarion Cycling Club.

A group of Blackburn Clarion cyclists, c 1910

Clarke was, for many years, a good friend of Blatchford's and rode with 'the Clarion' on some of their runs from Bolton. He describes a ride in 1900 to Nabs Farm, nearly Whalley, an early socialist 'club house' where he met up with members of the Clarion Club and Labour Church activists. However, the friendship with Blatchford did not last. They fell out over Blatchford's increasingly pro-war stance, a position that diminished Blatchford's popularity within the socialist movement as a whole. But 'The Clarion' movement lived on, becoming even more popular as a cycling club in the 1920s and 30s.[12]

---

[12] My late friend Denis Pye wrote a superb account of the club – *Fellowship is Life: The National Clarion Cycling Club 1895 – 1995,* Bolton 1995

Cotton Factory Times

TRADE UNION SECRETARIES—
Send Your Printing
TO THE
"Cotton Factory Times"
MARKET SQUARE, ASHTON-U-LYNE

2,646 VOLUME LI FRIDAY NOVEMBER 1, 1935 PRICE ONE PENNY

"In things essential, Unity; in things doubtful, Liberty; in all things, Charity." "Give me above all other liberties, the liberty to know, to utter, and to argue freely, according to conscience." — Milton.

DISEASES FROM DUST

Have the Tests on Grinders Been Adequate?

POSITION EXPLAINED

diseases are medically distinguishable from those among the ordinary population, or, to put it another way, that the disease is due, and it can medically be proved that it is due to some micro-organism peculiar to cotton dust. The words in black type are of supreme importance: we hoped from previous investigations, as well as the one in question, that the only barrier to the scheduling of the disease would be broken down. Our hopes have not been realised and, therefore, I repeat that 'from our point of view no positive results have been obtained.'

No Interference with Compensation

"It is important to remember, and should be obvious to anyone who takes an interest in this vital problem, that the investigation was an independent one and was carried out for the primary object of finding methods of prevention and cure. **It does not affect or interfere with our present attempt to obtain compensation for our disabled operatives.**

"The officials have done, and are doing, all they can to arrive at a satisfactory solution of this problem and are getting tired of this constant criticism which, oftener than not, is based on misapprehension and without regard to the difficulties of the situation. I would remind 'Cardroom Consumption' that the operatives have some responsibility for the present position, as was pointed out in the 'C.F.T.' Insurance Notes of last week and on many previous occasions. They should not be unmindful of the fact that advice has been given by the officials which they have ignored.

"One last point. In the last paragraph of your correspondent's letter, he states that two grinders have been treated very generously (sic), and goes on to say that

Misunderstanding

In the Heart of Anglezark

Our picture shows two keen Bolton mill girls who cycle all the year round. Like many others of their sex, they like a spin along country roads and over open moors after their week of hard work in the shed.

And a fine tonic it proves, strengthening to body and mind, a prophylactic against chills and colds. Here, during a brief spell of sunshine, they are seen resting on the Angelzark Moors, round by Rivington Pike.

Weaving Mills' Dispute

Ancilliary Workers' Wages

Weavers' Troubles

Complaints About New Wage List

The front cover of *The Cotton Factory Times* for November 1st 1935 showing a couple of young women cyclists having a break from the mill, enjoying a ride round Anglezark (sic)

Opening a wider world

Writing in 1898 he said: *"Cycling wonderfully widens the world of one who has been restricted to walking and railway riding; not alone does it open out new scenes, new places but introduces new characters of all sorts. It takes one into the tragedy and comedy of the highways and byways – town connections, rustic silences, wagons and carters in rural lanes, village greens and old fashioned inns..."* [13]

The bicycle opened a wider world for Clarke and his readers. Whilst *Moorlands and Memories* is often regarded as a purely 'Bolton' book, that is far from the case. On his faithful bike, Clarke takes us on excursions to Rossendale, Pendle, the Trough of Bowland, Windermere and the Yorkshire Dales. He even offers useful suggestions on the best routes to take, avoiding steep hills and getting the most scenic views. His writing is much more than descriptive. He is alert to landscape, people – and something more. Describing a ride to Lostock and Chew Moor, he writes in a style that Whitman would have recognised as similar to his own:

"I never go out but I see something, or hear something, of which I make a note –

[13] *Teddy Ashton's Journal* August 7th 1898

something to serve as a gem for a future tale or sketch. There is always something to see; always something to learn. Every new day makes revelations. I stretch out my soul into other men, their souls flow into mine – sometimes with dancing, sometimes with mourning."[14]

Clarke rode long distances on his bike – he went to Wembley with his friend Tom Hughes in 1924. Before the First World War he rode to Dorchester to meet Thomas Hardy (though he may have got the train part of the way). He would have disdained the modern fashion for figure-hugging lycra, preferring to ride in a tweed suit, with a green trilby and tie. His raincoat was usually fastened onto his handlebars.

Moorlands and Memories isn't his only cycling guide to Lancashire. *Windmill Land*, published slightly earlier, achieved for the Fylde what *Moorlands and Memories* does for the Lancashire moors. Both are much more than 'cycling' books – they are a delight to the walker, the lover of local history and culture and those with a spiritual side. Of course, you could be all of these and more. Clarke certainly was.

---

[14] *Moorlands* p.55

3. Our Lancashire moorlands since 1920

"What trivia things seem our great Empires and the history of man surveyed from the view-point of the stars that shine over the moors in the night. The fires on our hearths die out, the blaze of the glory of Empires fade away, and the pride and pomp of the great cities become only ruins and dust in the desert. But the stars shine on." [15]

Since Clarke was writing, during and after the First World War, the moors around Bolton have undergone much change but they remain a delight. The days of private landowners keeping the land to themselves as their personal playgrounds, have gone. Between the wars, most of the large estates passed into local authority ownership. But even bigger changes have swept through what Clarke called 'steam-engine land'. Not only is steam power confined to museums, the industry that steam drove – cotton – has vanished from Lancashire. But the moors endure.

Twilight of the mills: a disappearing landscape when this photo was taken in the 1980s

Yet one of the ironies of life in 2020 is that for many people the moors have become more, rather than less, difficult to access. Bus services have become few and far between, forcing people to either drive or go elsewhere. Fortunately, the modest railway station at Entwistle has survived, with an hourly train service between Manchester, Bolton and Blackburn, with the conveniently-situated 'Strawbury Duck' pub (formerly The Station Hotel) by the platform ramp.

[15] *Moorlands* p.337

Ownership of the moors

There have been big shifts in the ownership of the moors since Clarke was writing. Lord Leverhulme – a personal friend of Clarke's - handed over to Bolton Corporation much of the estate he purchased in 1900 to be used as a public park. However, Liverpool Corporation threw a spanner in the waterworks resulting in a lengthy tussle which led to Liverpool controlling much of the upland for its water supply. Leverhulme, helped by the talented landscape architect T. H. Mawson, developed the area that became 'Lever Park'. After his death in 1925 ownership of Leverhulme's part of the estate passed to John Magee, the brewer. When Magee died in 1939 the ideal solution would have been for Bolton Corporation to take over the entire estate but that didn't happen. Instead the park and the buildings fell into decay.[16]

As a result of national legislation passed during the Thatcher years, water was privatised and much of the Rivington estate passed to United Utilities. [17] Some of the worst forebodings of those opposed to water privatisation have not been realised and the company has worked with the local community to improve the estate. The most spectacular result of this co-operation has been the restoration of the gardens at Rivington, involving great input from the Friends of Rivington Gardens, Rivington Heritage Trust and The Conservation Volunteers. A substantial grant from the Heritage Lottery Fund has helped with the transformation (see Chapter 13).

To the east of Rivington lies the Smithills Estate. The land, as well as the historic Smithills Hall, passed into Bolton Corporation ownership in 1938. However, much of the estate remained inaccessible, at least legally. In the early 1980s interest developed in celebrating the Winter Hill 'Trespass' of 1896 and a well-attended march took place on the original 'trespass' route on September 5th 1982 (see Chapter 7). This stimulated interest in getting paths, already well-used by walkers, registered as rights-of-way.

Rivington Pike and the surrounding area is easily accessible on foot or by bike

[16] See M.D. Smith *Leverhulme's Rivington*, Bolton 1996

[17] For an excellent up to date history of Rivington and Anglezarke see Dave Lane, Derek Cartwiright and Garry Rhodes *Winter Hill and Anglezarke Scrapbook*, Bolton 2019.

The Woodland Trust

Sunset over Rivington, from The Two Lads cairn

In 2018 the Woodland Trust, a national charity, bought much of the estate, excluding the hall itself. Smithills is the largest of its expanding number of properties in the UK. Already, considerable effort has gone into improving the area for the benefit of all. It hasn't been without controversy; the car park at Walker Fold is regarded by some as an unsightly intrusion. But give it time, the shrubs and trees planted around it will mature and it could vie for the title of Bolton's prettiest car park, not that it would have much competition. And it's better than people parking on the verge, forcing walkers into the path of traffic.

Yes, it would be even better if people came on foot, bike or public transport. In the post-pandemic world, perhaps the humble bike will come back into its own, to much rejoicing from Allen Clarke, up there in his cycling heaven. I may be condemned as a philistine for saying this, but a good quality cafe wouldn't go amiss there, acting as a replacement for the fondly-remembered tea rooms at nearby Slack Hall. Then all it would need is a bus service to get people there and back.

The Winter Hill Fires

The recent history of the moors has not been without incident. On 28 June 2018, a fire broke out close to the television mast on Winter Hill, and a second fire was reported at the far east of the estate the next day. By 30th June, the two fires had merged, engulfing the top of Smithills Estate in flames. Emergency services and helicopters were drafted in to dampen the flames but it was not finally declared out until 9th August 2018. Considerable damage had been done to the site. About 31% of the area was affected and the fire had a huge impact on wildlife. Nesting birds, insects, frogs, toads, lizards and rodents were all caught in the blaze, many species perishing in the fire.

The 2018 fires: Greater Manchester Fire and Rescue Service battle with the flames above Rivington. *Photo courtesy Ben Earlam*

Moorland is used to fire and so should recover in time, allowing animals from surrounding areas to re-colonise. But it will take some years. Writing in late May 2020, the moors are once again ablaze after weeks without rain, caused by inconsiderate picnickers.

But getting back to our guide and inspiration, Allen Clarke. He would have recognised today's moors and rejoiced that they still exist to enjoy. I can only echo his call to make the most of them, *"finding in our moorlands and their memories health for the body, happiness for the heart, and vision for the soul."*[18]

The view from the north side of Winter Hill...."*health for the body, happiness for the heart, vision for the soul*"

---

[18] *Moorlands* p.341

4. Starting out from Platform 4

"Whitsuntide is the great Lancashire holiday season. Then, dozens of railway trains rush seawards with thousands of noisy, merry operatives of all sorts and conditions. Ere the sun has arisen cheap trips are cleaving through the dawn; and long after the sun has set at night the heavy-laden trains are returning home one by one." [19]

What better place to start our journey than Bolton's Trinity Street station, from the Blackpool-bound Platform 4? Generations of Boltonians have departed from here - on holiday, to seek work, or go to war. Today, we mostly 'commute'. Clarke writes a lot about Bolton ('Spindleton') station, as a place of excitement and departure – picturing families, friends and lovers taking the train to Blackpool. In his novel *The Knobstick* he sets the scene for a lovers' excursion - a 'cheap trip' to Blackpool at Whitsun, before the days of week-long 'holidays with pay'.

It's Whit Friday; the hero and heroine – Harry Belton and Lizzie Banks – arrive at Bolton station amongst a large throng of excursionists, all heading for Blackpool. The train comes to a stop and Harry joins the rush: *"He got in the train, after much crushing, with the Banks's and sat next to Lizzie. Every carriage was packed; and the railway platform was a dense mass of merry, jostling people, with a noisy sprinkling of squalling babies and chattering children."* [20]

In the last years of steam, an ex-LMS 'Black 5' departs from Platform 4 on a train for the coast, July 1967

---

[19] *The Knobstick: a tale of labour and love*, Bolton 1893 p.116

[20] *The Knobstick* p.123

Today, most Boltonians travelling to Blackpool and Southport will join their train on the same Platform 4 as Harry and Lizzie did. Although the Refreshment Room is only a memory, the station buildings are being brought back to use by the station's community partnership, with an art gallery and meeting rooms. I think Allen Clarke would have approved. His most well-loved poem, 'A Gradely Prayer' is displayed at the north end of Platform 4, together with 'To a Locomotive in Winter' by Walt Whitman. A real ale bar is planned for Platform 4 as well.

Another 'Chep Trip to Blackpool'

Clarke returns to a more detailed description of a 'chep (cheap) trip' from Bolton to Blackpool in a later novel, *Lancashire Lasses and Lads*, published in 1906. Once again, two lovers – Dick and Hannah – are the focus of attention, although they are part of a larger family group. The locomotive whistles as it departs, "*puffing under the snappy series of short tunnels leading westward and seawards out of the great manufacturing town*." [21]

The train gains speed and heads towards 'Crostock' (Lostock) Junction, passing the large mill (Heaton's) that once occupied the site to the south of the line, now a housing estate. Clarke brings in a bit of social observation, through 'Mary Ann', the younger sister of Hannah:

"Hello, we'n just gone under Lady Bridge, an' theer's Giant's Cheer, see yo'. That bit o' stone delph just in th'shape of a cheer; an' here's Crostock factory, th' only factory abeaut Spindleton where there's yet women 'mindin'' in th' spinnin'-reaum. Shame on 'em, say I; an' here's Crostock Junction, an' we're not stoppin', but gooin' straight through." [22]

A view of the station gardens and Junction Hotel, November 1966. The day the station closed. Heaton's Mill is in the background

---

[21] *The Knobstick* p.160

[22] *The Knobstick* p.161

After Lostock Junction the view opens up towards Rivington Pike , part of "*a range of mooryhills, one of which, shaped somewhat like the back of an elephant, the resemblance being suggested and strengthened by the fact that a small stone tower (like the elephant and castle in the Spindleton coat of arms) crowned the peak in the centre of the mountain, was greatest and most conspicuous*." [23]

Beeching Reversed at Lostock

You can see the same view today, on a faster and quieter electric train. The railway from Manchester via Bolton to Preston was electrified early in 2019. Lostock Junction station is no longer called 'junction' and for a period of over 20 years had no station at all. It was closed as part of the 'Beeching' cuts on November 5th 1966, to much letting-off of fireworks and detonators. The story of that 'last train' is a tale in itself. The stopping train was running late and the Glasgow-Manchester express ran ahead of it. The fast train hit the 30 or so detonators that had been laid on the track to mark 'the last train' and came to a very quick stop beyond the signalbox. The express went on its way and the now-delayed 'stopper' trundled in behind it, to collect a group of subdued revellers.

But it was an unhappy day for the local community and perhaps particularly sad for the friendly Asian stationmaster, Mr Moosa Atcha. He was redeployed elsewhere on the railway but must have missed the 'country' feel of the station back then, and the lovely flower beds he tended.

Mr Moosa Atcha was the last stationmaster/porter at Lostock Junction. He came from a small village called Barbodhan near Rangoon (Burma)

[23] *The Knobstick* p.162

There's a happy ending of sorts. The 'Preston side' platforms were re-opened in 1988 and the station has never been busier. Transport for Greater Manchester has aspirations to expand the station and re-instate the Wigan platforms. What's more, plans are afoot by a local business partnership to re-open the adjacent long-empty Lostock Arms (formerly 'The Junction Hotel'). Can't wait.

Clarke often cycled past Lostock Junction station and in *Moorlands and Memories* he describes a ride from Bolton through Markland Hill and down Lostock Junction Lane. It's typical Clarke – jumping from the everyday to deep philosophical musing:

"I cross the railway bridge (there is a train off to Blackpool – I think of the dear old sea) and pedal up a stiff hill. Half way up I pass a little school; the children are at play in the yard. What a noise! - skipping rope, marbles, tops. Is there any merrier sight in the world than a lot of children at play? These be future angels (I think), or future -; no, we do not believe in hell. On such a day as this we cannot believe in eternal punishment, we can only believe in a good God who will somehow, some day, bring all souls to peace and heaven."[24]

Views from a carriage window

A short distance further on, near to where Clarke's excursionists looked out to Rivington Pike, there is the new station of Horwich Parkway serving the vast Middlebrook retail park and football ground. In Clarke's day you could look out on the long series of smoking workshops that made up Horwich Loco Works. It closed in 1983 but demolition only began in 2019 to make way for a large housing development.

People still travel to Blackpool for a day out, making the most of the new, fast electric trains which I'm sure Clarke would have liked for their environmental advantages as well as comfort. He was very much a 'green' before his time and bemoaned the polluting mills that he grew up amongst.

In his novel *A Daughter of the Factory* the heroine Rose tells her lover, Frank, as they stand together on a hillside overlooking the polluted town of 'Slagbourne': *"Ah Frank, there is much to do to make this world bright and clean....We must make Lancashire clean again. We must wash the smoky dust off the petals of the red rose."*[25]

---

[24] *Moorlands* p.55

[25] *Teddy Ashton's Northern Weekly*, October 29th 1898

The Horwich Jerk and another last train

Let's leave the 'cheap trip', making a special stop at Blackrod before returning back to Bolton. It would be good if the little station had more to offer. Some neighbouring stations, including Westhoughton, Adlington, Hindley and others, have hard-working volunteer 'friends' groups who have transformed dull and lifeless places into amazing spaces with gardens and art work. Blackrod would benefit from its own 'friends', perhaps celebrating its history as the station where the local 'Horwich Jerk' connected with incoming trains, taking people up the short branch to Horwich.

For many years the branch was worked by a Lancashire and Yorkshire Railway 'Rail Motor' – essentially a small locomotive and a passenger carriage combined, allowing the driver to operate the controls from the carriage end, like a modern-day railcar. The fireman stayed on the footplate and made sure the fire was looked after and the boiler kept full. It became known as 'The Jerk' because of its jerky movement when operating 'in reverse'.

Last train from Horwich: September 25th 1965
Photo courtesy Vern Sidlow

Horwich was another victim of the Beeching cuts of the 1960s, closing a year before Lostock Junction on September 25th 1965. The last train was hauled by specially-cleaned Bolton 'tank' locomotive number 42626. A few of us spent many evenings before the 'last day' cleaning her up in Crescent Road sheds. The final day, a Saturday, was wet and miserable but a crowd of some 200 gave the last train – the 12.15 to Bolton – a rousing send-off. The driver was Bob Croston, who kindly allowed several of us enthusiasts to ride in the cab through to Bolton.

Attempts in the 1990s to re-open the railway into Horwich itself (The 'Horwich Rail Link' campaign) didn't come to fruition, but at least there is Horwich Parkway, though it's a hefty walk from the town itself and without a direct bus link.

5. Up Halliwell Road

"Let us, then, go up Halliwell Road towards the moors...Once upon a time it must have been a bonny moorland road..."[26]

I'd say there are five very special roads leading out of Bolton: Deane Road and Derby Street (which becomes St Helen's Road) heading south-west; Tonge Moor Road going north, Halliwell Road heading north-westerly and Chorley Old Road going further westward. Why are they 'special'? It's because of their history but also their present-day character. All are very lively, multi-cultural, places. Chorley New Road with its pretentious gated 'residences' doesn't compare. Manchester Road has lost most of its character since the Wanderers moved out and retail parks moved in.

Of all of them, I like Haliiwell Road the best. I have the good fortune of living right at the top of it, where inner-urban Bolton has a brief flirtation with suburbia before opening up to the moors above Smithills.

In Clarke's day, you could take a tram (Route 'H' for Halliwell) up to the Ainsworth Arms. They ran every few minutes, unlike our half-hourly bus service today. Moss Bank Way didn't exist; it was only constructed in the 1930s. The gated Forest Road, owned by Colonel Ainsworth, linked up with Halliwell Road and Harpers Lane. To the annoyance of Solomon Partington, whom we will meet soon, bicycles and 'perambulators' were forbidden. But let's go back to the beginning, or even earlier, to the town centre.

One of the friezes at Sunnyside Mills, Daubhill, before they were taken down and re-erected as part of the Market Place development

The Market Hall is a good place to start. Many regret the loss of the market stalls and the new 'Market Place' is a bit of a curate's egg, though the most recent additions (including The Light cinema) are very good. Inside the shopping area there's some Lancashire dialect sayings on the walls; maybe a 'Teddy Ashton' poem should be on display! A special feature of the Market Place is the series of stone friezes rescued from Sunnyside Mills, Daubhill, when the factory was being demolished. They are just by the bus stops on Bridge Street.

---

[26] *Moorlands* pp.111-2

There's an Allen Clarke connection here. In 1906 there was a prolonged strike at Sunnyside over the introduction of new looms. The mostly female weavers were expected to work more looms for much the same money. Clarke, in his paper *Teddy Ashton's Northern Weekly*, published a series of sketches ('Th' Dobbill Do') about the 'patent automatic cemetery looms', so called because they would work the weavers to an early grave. He (probably) wrote under the pseudonym of 'Billy Pickinpeg' and in his characteristic way used humour to make a serious point (see Chapter 22).

In the early years of his publishing career, most of Clarke's newspapers and books and pamphlets were printed at Pendlebury's printing shop at 54 Higher Bridge Street. His hugely popular *Tum Fowt Sketches*, featuring the adventures of Bill and Bet Spriggs, were produced here in their thousands at 1d a copy.

Embarrassment on Higher Bridge Street

Higher Bridge Street is much changed even 'sin' aw were a lad'. I used to cycle this way to school, often passing a couple of mill girls at the bus stop. They always used to cheer me on with shouts of "come on lad, you're winning!" It was all very embarrassing. The 'Wryton' wrestling stadium is gone, as well as some of the big mills such as Holdsworth's. Moss Street Baths, another place of torture as far as I was concerned, is long demolished. It was situated a short way further up after the elegant Grecian Mill, which still survives as a storage warehouse.

Things start to get interesting again at the junction of the two main roads. Let's leave Blackburn Road to its own devices and head up Halliwell Road. But before we go too far, remember that the junction was where the great 'Winter Hill Mass Trespass' marches of September 1896 began. The first started with a few hundred folk, addressed by local socialists and radicals. By the time it got to the Ainsworth Arms it was 10,000 strong.

There's a fascinating tramway survival a few yards up from where Halliwell Road starts. In his book Clarke talks about 'taking tram' up Halliwell Road, as well as using these 'gondolas of the people' to reach other destinations. Look out for the last surviving lamp post that once carried the electric cables for the Halliwell tram. It is maintained by local volunteers, though nobody has any idea as to who actually owns it!

Another fascinating souvenir of the Halliwell tram came to light in 2019 when roadworks revealed substantial lengths of tram rail. After the trams ceased operation, Bolton Corporation simply tarmaced over the rails in many cases, rather than going to the expense of having them removed. It's a shame that the trams no longer rattle up and down Halliwell Road. They finished in 1947. When some major roadworks were being done in 2019 several lengths of tram rail were uncovered by the contractors and some are now in the safe keeping of Halliwell Local History Society.[27]

Exiled: Bolton's refugees and asylum seekers

Clarke has quite a lot to say about Halliwell Road in *Moorlands and Memories*. He talks about 'Owd Shappey' who was a refugee who fled the French Revolution of the 1790s. Was he Bolton's first asylum-seeker? Perhaps that distinction belongs to the Huguenot weavers. But 'Owd Shappey' was a bit of a rarity. He ended up in Barrow Bridge but then moved down and *"spent the rest of his life on one side or other of this Halliwell Road."*

Clarke was naturally sympathetic towards refugees – his father and grandfather fled Ireland during the Potato Famine of the 1840s. He says *"What a sad thing it must be to be a compulsory exile, fleeing to save your life, even if you find such a sweet harbour as Barrow Bridge."*[28]

Another refugee who added colour to Halliwell Road was the owner of 'Pedro's Taverna' - Pedro Cuadrado, a refugee from the Spanish Civil War who ran his bar on Halliwell Road up to the 1990s. His sangria and hot beef sandwiches were legendary. He died in 2010 at the age of 88.Today, Halliwell Road and its surroundings are home to many more refugees and asylum seekers, adding a very cosmopolitan feel to this road to the moors.

Pedro and his celebrated Taverna, for many years a feature on Halliwell Road. Photo courtesy Sue Hamer

---

27 See the splendid history of Bolton's trams by Derek Shepherd and Tony Young *Bolton Tramways*, 2019.

28 *Moorlands* pp.112-3

Clarke would have been fascinated by the multi-cultural 'buzz' of Halliwell Road. On the site of the old Prospect Mill is the Noor-al-Masjid mosque, one of Bolton's largest places of worship. Continue up the hill and there are shops and takeaways from successive generations of immigrants and refugees: Asian, complemented by Hungarians, Poles and others.

The view down Halliwell Road in the early 1980s. Pedro's is on the left (you can just about see him sat down outside); Prospect Mill towers beyond

Streets of culture and romance

It's surprising how little the area has changed. Many of the mills have gone but the streets are still there. Clarke has quite a bit to say about them. He tells us that he went to Mount Street School where his 'scribbling instincts' broke out and notes that *"the streets in this region all bearing famous and classic names poets, musicians, painters etc. – Homer, Virgil, Cellini, Raphael, Rossini, Wagner, Carlyle, Tennyson, Mozart, Angelo etc.; Halliwell is the one part of Bolton notable for its romantic street nomenclature – though one must admit that the artistic persons whose names adorn the street signs would hardly go into raptures over some of the places in the locality."* [29]

So take it from me – and Allen Clarke - Halliwell Road is well worth exploring. The days when you could visit something like 20 pubs within a mile are long gone, but those that remain have character. Tucked away to the east of Halliwell Road is 'The

---

[29] *Moorlands* p.114

Weavers' Arms', better known as 'Th'Mop' or even 'Th'Frozzen Mop'[30].

You can get most of life's necessities along Halliwell Road, from a pint to fish and chips or a curry, freshly-baked pies and 'flour cakes' (Boltonese for 'barm cakes'), a book of stamps, haircut, water butt or dry cleaning. But, if you've got the stamina, don't ignore The Ainsworth Arms, Lord Raglan, Last Orders, The Crofters Arms and The Stork. And, of course, The Mop.

Falcon Mill today

[30] The Yew Tree Inn, Anglezarke, used to be known by locals as 'The Frozen Mop' as well, according to George Birtill in *The Enchanted Hills* (1966)

6. On to Smithills and The Halliwell Moors

"If instead of going to the left for Barrow Bridge you keep on up the steep hill, Brian Hey, you come to the gates of Smithills Hall – venerable with antiquity and interesting with history. It is said that a thousand years ago it was a Saxon palace, the abode of King Ella, at a time when in the moorland woods packs of wolves prowled and the hall was walled round to keep the beasts out...We live in comparatively tame times don't we, eh? Yet I don't know. They may have had wolves in the old times, but they never had anything like our amazing inventions, not to mention the Greatest War ever known, with all its heroism and horror. I rather fancy that the sight of an aeroplane would have scared the Saxon serfs as aver a wolf did, and a motor car, or even an electric tram running up Halliwell Road, would have made them take to their heels as much as any wild beast."[31]

The upper part of Halliwell Road was originally called 'Water Street' before becoming Pilkington Street at the top. If you look out on the right hand side as you go up, you will find the 'Water Street' name embedded in one of the terraced cottages. The Hill Top area remains a fascinating pre-industrial community of handloom weavers' cottages, overshadowed by Falcon Mill, one of the best remaining examples of Bolton's cotton spinning heritage. Let's hope it doesn't go the way of so many others. [32]

The jolly celebration of the 1896 Winter Hill 'Mass Trespass', approaching the Ainsworth Arms with Eagley Band in the lead and a good following of local kids. Not sure what the Colonel would have thought...

---

[31] *Moorlands* p.116

[32] See Margaret Koppens' useful walks booklet *Halliwell Road and Hill Top*, published by Halliwell Local History Society, 2001

Old Halliwell

Cross the busy Moss Bank Way and drop down into the dip before reaching the Smithills schools. For now, ignore Allen Clarke's instruction to continue up the road and turn left along Smithills Croft Road and you'll see what little remains of the bleachworks and the location of the 'Holy Well' that gave 'Halliwell' its' name. Most of the bleachworks site is now housing. If you turn right where the road curves sharply to the left, there's a pleasant walk up a cobbled path through the woods – you can get to Barrow Bridge that way eventually.

Returning on to Smithills Dean Road, from here it's a continuous climb of varying degrees of severity, up to Brian Hey. Smithills Hall is to the right and is one of those special places in Bolton that should be visited. Clarke has much to say about it in *Moorlands and Memories* and it has changed little over the last century; it is now owned by Bolton Council and has informative displays on the history of the hall. It also has a very good tea room and the cakes are to die for. Gradually, Bolton Council and Friends of Smithills Hall volunteers are bringing the gardens back into a good state.

Further up 'The Dean' there are remains of coal mining, developed by the Ainsworths. There were tramways built to move coal from the local pits; on the dirt track to Horrocks Fold there was a replica of an old chaldron wagon, though it suffered serious damage during 2019. I hope it can be restored and put back on its original short section of rail.

A grand view

It's a hard pull for a cyclist, at least if you're as unfit as I am. Clarke said *"this Brian Hey is a stiff climb even for pedestrians and is a tough proposition for a cyclist. But I have ridden up it and feel proud of the feat, and so has My Lady, and she, hampered by skirts, may feel still more pride in the achievement."* [33] Well good for you, Teddy. Anyway, I can report that I sail up in comfort on my electric bike; maybe that's cheating, but I don't care.

At the junction of Smithills Dean Road and Scout Road it's compulsory to stop and take in the view. Clarke waxed lyrical. *"From the top of Brian Hey you have a wide and wondrous view. It is pleasant to sit on the wooden form, considerately set there, and look and muse on the prospect. Down below is the big town, behind are the moorlands."* [34]

---

[33] *Moorlands* p.116

[34] *Moorlands* p.118

And good that the 'wooden bench' remains, though maybe it isn't the same that graced the site in 1920. In fact, the bench flourishes, in the care of an elderly chap – Tommy - from Halliwell (Cloister Street) who comes up most days to wave at passing motorists, horse-riders and cyclists. He has become an institution. Just to the right along Scout Road is Brian Hey Farm. For many years it had a lovely traditional tea room which did the most delicious home-made scones with jam and cream. Today it still offers a very good service for ice-cream lovers, self included.

If you turn left along Scout Road, heading towards Walker Fold, look out for the ancient milestone on the left of the road. And further on, you'll find 'Colliers Row' and 'New Colliers' Row' highlighting the area's mining heritage.

Tommy on his bench with a couple of lady friends

Talking Tolstoy: Burnt Edge, Walker Fold and Eighteen Acre Farm

If you continue across Scout Road, following in the footsteps of the Winter Hill rights-of-way demonstrators of 1896, you'll get to the gate which the huge throng besieged. Resist the temptation to head through the gate and on towards Winter Hill, but stop to salute the memory of 1896, celebrated on the 'Trespass Stone' erected a century later. It's a great view across Bolton from here.

Continue along the tarmac road passing Gilligant's Farm and you'll approach Holden's Farm. If you follow the public footpath round the side of the farm you'll soon enter Woodland Trust land, with its' welcoming sign. A little bit further on you'll come to somewhere very special – the ruins of Eighteen Acre Farm. It was here in the summer of 1904 that Allen Clarke and a party of over 50 men, women and children from Bolton Labour Church stopped off on one of their 'Sunday Afternoon Walks'. Clarke says "*we argued socialism, Tolstoyanism, and many other 'isms' before standing to sing Edward Carpenter's hymn:*

England arise! The long, long night is over

Faint in the east, before the dawn appear..."[35]

---

[35] In *Northern Weekly*, August 6th 1904

The farm was abandoned decades ago, but the ruins are clearly visible. Next time you walk by, stop off a few minutes to sing 'England Arise!' You'll feel so much better for it.

After bursting into song, you could continue up the path and come onto the Winter Hill Road, close to the long-demolished 'Five Houses' which once featured an ale-house and revolutionary conspiracies, so Clarke suggests. But you can read about that in the next chapter. Be patient! Instead, turn left at the junction of the paths, close to the farm ruins. This track takes you to Burnt Edge and the site of the old colliery and brickworks. They had ceased to operate even in Clarke's day, but there are some signs of their existence. A couple of mine shafts have been capped (don't go too near) and there are remains of kilns.

There are a couple of options for walkers. I'd recommend continuing the modest climb up on to Burnt Edge itself where there are magnificent views not only across to Winter Hill but further afield towards Rossendale. I often go this way on my bike (it's permitted but please respect walkers and give them priority).

There are some conveniently-placed benches along 'The Edge'. Why not stop awhile and take in the view? Carry on past the delightfully-named Slack Hall, which was once a tea room not so long ago. We need to revive the old Lancashire 'tea room' tradition and make the most of those that survive.

Instead of veering off to the right, follow the footpath straight on and you'll join with another path coming up from the valley. You will emerge above Walker Fold, with more wonderful views towards Bolton and Manchester. Continue down the path by the new Woodland Trust car park and you come out at Walker Fold itself – you are back on Scout Road. This is an ancient settlement but its fascination for me - and Allen Clarke - is the Walt Whitman connection.

Walker Fold and Walt Whitman

The large, rustic-style house at the corner of the small settlement (or 'fold') was the home of John Ormrod, part of the Bolton mill-owning dynasty but also a very active member of the Walt Whitman 'Fellowship'. In the later years of the Whitman group, Ormrod played host to the annual 'Whitman Day' picnics on or near to May 31st. J. W. Wallace, the 'master' of the Bolton Whitman group and friend of Clarke's, gave one of his last and most philosophical speeches to the annual Whitman Day gathering here in 1925, on the subject of 'If Walt Whitman Came to Walker Fold'.

In the late 1920s and early 1930s Ormrod visited American Whitman enthusiasts during business trips to the States, meeting people such as John Burroughs, the famous naturalist and friend of Whitman's. He also had friendships with several American anarchists who were inspired by Whitman.[36]

From here, walk through the finely-restored cottages in Walker Fold and pick up the path which takes you down to Barrow Bridge and the 63 Steps.

There's an hourly bus back into Bolton, during the week. You will pass the site of an old farmhouse called 'Twitchell's' or 'Twitchems' which used to do a popular (and illegal) trade in selling home-brewed ('whoam-brewed' in gradely Lancashire) ale. [37] It has become traditional for the annual Walt Whitman Walk to stop here for a breather and some poetry readings. Chris Chilton, chair of Bolton Socialist Club which leads the annual walk, has written fine poem called 'Whitman in the Woods':

> *"We climb sixty three steps up an old miners'*
> *Path towards the peat-covered moors that*
> *Colliers burrowed into for something*
> *Resembling a living, arriving breathless*
> *At the top to gather in a clearing beneath*
> *A black-barked scrag of a tree that has*
> *Shouldered single-mindedly through the*
> *Tangled mess of shoots and shrubs in its quest*
> *For growth and light and a more substantial life...."*[38]

---

[36] The story is told in more detail in my book *With Walt Whitman in Bolton*, 3rd edition, Bolton 2019

[37] See Derek Billington and Clive Walsh *Barrow Bridge*, Halliwell Local History Society, 1998

[38] Chris Chilton 'Whitman in the Woods' in *How to Count Trees and other poems*, Bolton 2020

7. Will Yo' Come O' Sunday Mornin'? - The Winter Hill 'Trespass'

"Ay, the moors lie round Bolton like a magic mantle; a magic mantle from the Goddess Hygiene; and there be those who would take this mantle, the people's property, from those who have every right to it."[39]

Asserting ancient rights

Keep trudging up Smithills Dean Road and cross busy Scout Road, with care. You're now on Coalpit Road, harking back to the mining that was once extensive around here. Most of it had gone by the 1920s though remains are still to be seen in the form of small slag heaps. You are walking in the footsteps of some very special people.

Clarke writes *"Wolves have been mentioned as prowling round these regions in olden time. No doubt they were a pest and a danger, but one wonders if they were as much a nuisance as some of our modern gentry, who enclose lands and bar people from footpaths over the moors."*

He continues *"On Sunday September 6th, 1896, ten thousand Boltonians marched up this Brian Hey to pull down a gate and protest against a footpath to Winter Hill being claimed and closed by the landlord."* [40]

The crowd surged up Smithills Dean and then along Coalpit Road until they reached the gate, which had been closed off by the landowner, Colonel Ainsworth. There was a melee and the gate was smashed. Thousands of demonstrators burst onto the disputed road and carried on over Winter Hill and down to Belmont, where they were said to have had a great time in The Wright's Arms, drinking the pub dry. The Black Dog did an equally brisk trade.

The 1982 march, heading up Coalpit Road towards Winter Hill on September 5th

---

[39] Allen Clarke 'Right of Road – What about Winter Hill?' editorial in *Teddy Ashton's Northern Weekly*, September 30th 1899

[40] *Moorlands* p.119

The demonstrations continued over three more weekends, as well as on a Wednesday afternoon to permit shop workers to attend on their afternoon off. The following week it was estimated that 12,000 joined the march, which was unimpeded by police or gamekeepers. Meetings were held in Bolton to raise support for the campaign. If the public was on the side of the campaigners, the law wasn't. The court case brought by Ainsworth against the 'ringleaders' – mostly local socialists like Joe Shufflebotham of Astley Bridge, but also the venerable radical Liberal, Solomon Partington – was successful. Although nobody went to jail, they had to pay heavy fines, most of which was covered by public contributions.

Clarke's book was important in keeping alive the memory of what happened in 1896 – probably Britain's biggest ever 'mass trespass', far eclipsing Kinder Scout of 1932. Although, it must be stressed, those thousands of Boltonians didn't regard themselves as 'trespassing' at all – they were reclaiming their rights that had been arrogantly usurped.[41]

It's interesting that both events were organised, in the main, by local left-wing activists. In 1896 it was Bolton branch of the Social Democratic Federation, fore-runner of the Communist Party of Great Britain, whose members organised the Kinder Trespass. I was able to show Benny Rothman, leader of the Kinder Trespass, the site of the Winter Hill events in 1982; he joined us on the commemorative march later that year.

Leader of the 1932 Kinder Scout Trespass, Benny Rothman, 50 years later, pictured with the author at the colonel's 'shooting hut' on the disputed road to Winter Hill, August 1982

[41] For the full story see my *Will Yo' Come O' Sunday Mornin? The 1896 Battle for Winter Hill*, Bolton 1982 and Huddersfield 1996

Re-discovery

The revival of interest in the Winter Hill 'trespass' came about through a talk at Bolton Socialist Club early in 1982. It was suggested we should organise a commemoration later that year on the nearest Sunday to when the demonstration occurred, which was September 5th. The Socialist Club and Bolton branch of the Workers Educational Association helped to set up a committee which made preparations for the march. A play was written by Les Smith which was performed in pubs and clubs around Bolton, including several on Halliwell Road, in the run up to the commemorative march.

Some of the 1982 demonstration, negotiating the gully which was once crossed by a bridge. Jim Taylor pictured on left (with rucksack). Harvey Scowcoft, with cap, assisting people across the stream

On the day, about a thousand people assembled at the bottom of Halliwell Road, where the original march had begun. We set off to the tune of 'The Happy Wanderer' performed by Eagley Band and picked up several more recruits as we headed up towards Brian Hey – mostly local kids. It was interesting to discover recently that the famous Bolton-born actor Maxine Peake was on that march, as a tiny eight-year old accompanied by her step-grandad Jim Taylor.

The centenary of the demonstrations was marked by another march, in September 1996 and a stone plaque was erected by the gate. It includes the words 'Will Yo' Come O' Sunday Morning?' a reference to Allen Clarke's song, published in his paper *Teddy Ashton's Journal* following the first demonstration. The chorus goes:

> *"Will yo' come o' Sunday mornin'*
> *For a walk o'er Winter Hill?*
> *Ten thousand went last Sunday*
> *But there's room for thousand still!*
> *Oh there moors are rare and bonny*
> *And the heather's sweet and fine*
> *And the roads across the hilltops –*
> *Are the people's – yours and mine!"*[42]

The original music was lost in the mists of time and Winter Hill but musician Nat Clare put his own music to it and performed the song, with gusto, at many venues around Bolton in the run-up to the 1982 celebration.

Solomon Partington

Allen Clarke described him 'as disinterested a champion of liberty and justice as ever used a pen on behalf of the robbed and oppressed'. Solomon Partington was one of the key figures in the Winter Hill 'Trespass' - but let's not call it a 'trespass' as the people who marched saw themselves not as 'trespassers' but honest law-abiding people claiming their rights. In the court case that followed the 'events' of September 1896 he was ordered to pay costs of £300, most of which was covered by public subscription.

Solomon Partington

He was a journalist, born in Middleton and moved to Leigh to edit the local paper in 1887. He was promoted to a senior job on *The Bolton Evening News* in the early 1890s. Partington was a staunch Liberal of the Gladstonian pro-Irish Home Rule school. He made common cause with the local socialists in Bolton over the Winter Hill issue and after the events of 1896 devoted himself to a campaign for access to the moorland around Winter Hill and Smithills. He produced a series of six 'Truth' pamphlets arguing the case for public rights of way. In 1904 he was elected on to Bolton Council, running on an independent 'public rights' platform supported by Clarke and his *Northern Weekly*.

---

[42] *Teddy Ashton's Journal*, September 19th 1896

He served the people of West Ward (Halliwell and Smithills) until 1911, with a year's break in 1907. He was a key figure in the Bolton Municipal Reform League, together with his socialist friend Sarah Reddish, with whom he shared a common passion for the principles and practice of co-operation. He wrote the history of Middleton Co-operative Society.

Partington shared Clarke's love of the Lancashire dialect and was a member of the Lancashire Authors' Association which Clarke set up in 1909. After his move to Silverdale, and then Grange-over-Sands, Partington devoted himself to historical research though he never completed his intended 'magnum opus' - a history of Lancashire dialect writing. His two books on the dialect, *The Future of Old English Words* and *Romance of the Dialect,* show what might have been achieved.

Winter Hill then and now

You can now walk over Winter Hill without fear of prosecution. When you get to the gate, salute those thousands of Boltonians who asserted their rights over those of the landowner's. It's a fairly easy walk all the way up to Winter Hill from here, though strong footwear is recommended. The further you go, the better the view becomes. You pass the site of the recently-demolished Ainsworth's shooting hut on the left, beyond the steep gully which was once crossed by a bridge. Remains of ancient coal pits are dotted about the place.

If it's clear, you will see the masts of Winter Hill ahead of you. The path deviates slightly but make sure you pass 'Scotchman's Stump' – the home-made memorial to Henderson, the 'Scotch traveller' who died while crossing the moor in 1838. It reads: *"In memory of George Henderson, traveller, native of Annan, Dumfrieshire, who was barbarously murdered on Horwich Moor, on Monday November 9th, 1838 in the 20th year of his age."* Henderson was a 'packman', or commercial traveller, who was walking from Blackrod to the Black Dog Inn, Belmont, where he had arranged to meet a friend. His body was found in a ditch by a local lad, who sought help from local miners to retrieve the body.

In Clarke's description, he uses 'Arran' instead of 'Annan'. Perhaps an easy mistake for an Englishman to make. He notes that *"this tragedy is one of the instances where 'murder did not out' – at least in this world. The culprit was never discovered."*[43] A local man, James Whittle, was arrested and sent for trial. He lived in 'Five Houses', which stood on the track running down from Winter Hill to Horwich. He was acquitted. Henderson may well have been the victim of a shooting accident, but nobody will ever be certain.

---

43 *Moorlands* p.120

The story of the memorial is part of the romance of Winter Hill. The 'stump' was taken from a cotton mill in Halliwell – it's a typical example of the pillars used in 19th century spinning mills. It was dragged up to Winter Hill by a group of friends – Tom Hutchinson (son of William Hutchinson, a leading figure in the 1896 trespass), B.F. Davies and his brother Don Davies. The new memorial, erected in 1912, replaced a previous one and was intended to be a commemoration of the 1896 events and an indication that there was a right of way.[44]

Don – or 'Donny' - Davies was a highly acclaimed sportsman, both a cricketer and footballer, who went on to become *The Manchester Guardian's* chief football correspondent. Tragically, he died in the Munich Air Disaster in 1958.

A 1912 photo of Scotchman's Stump following the erection of a new 'pillar'. The stump came from a mill in Halliwell and was dragged up Winter Hill by a team of enthusiastic (and strong) volunteers, to show respect for the murdered packman but also to demonstrate there was a right of way over Winter Hill. *Courtesy Geoff Hutchinson*

The moors around Winter Hill have had more than their fair share of aviation disasters. The first took place in the 1920s when a plane crashed into the hill.

---

[44] See *Will Yo' Come O' Sunday Mornin'?* p.12. For a full account of the shooting and the trial of James Whittle, see David Holding *Murder in the Heather: The Winter Hill Murder of 1838*, Bolton 1991. Also 'Winter Hill: Heath of Death and Mystery' by Gordon Readyhough, *Lancashire Magazine*, November 1979.

Others occurred during the Second World War including a US Air Force plane that came off course. Six RAF crew members were killed when their Wellington bomber crashed near Rivington on November 12th 1943. A small memorial exists to the tragedy, above Lead Mines Clough. Near to the top of Winter Hill is a memorial to the passengers on a plane from the Isle of Man to Manchester which crashed on 27th February 1958 killing 35 people.

The story of 'Scotchman's Stump' forms part of the mystery and romance of Winter Hill. It has never been as popular as Rivington Pike, but, as Clarke tells us, the views are magnificent, stretching across to Southport, Wigan and Blackpool with its famous tower. If you're lucky, you might see Snowdonia and the Isle of Man. Clarke's exuberant but heartfelt celebration of the view remains every bit as true today as it was in 1920:

"Sit down here, on a summer's day, on the green moorland under the blue sky, and though you own not a yard of land nor a stick of property, you are on a throne, and king of the world – a happier and far more innocent king than any ruler who ever held tinsel court and played havoc with the destiny of nations – you are monarch of all the magic of the moorlands, of healthy air for the lungs, of Nature's pictures for the eye, of Nature's music for the ear..." [45]

Two other monarchs of the moorland....

---

[45] *Moorlands* p.121

8. Barrow Bridge is still bonny (so is Barrowbridge)

"I remember Barrow Bridge when it was really 'the deserted village' – when only one or two cottages by the brook were tenanted, when all the houses up to the village green and institute were empty, with rotting windows and doors, and grass growing on the doorsteps, where the bleak bare mills stood like giant skeleton surveying a scene of desolation and decay."[46]

Of all places in Lancashire, Clarke loved Barrow Bridge most of all. He called it *"perhaps the most beloved of all the rural haunts around Bolton"* – adding *"It is to me, anyhow."* And me!

But just to start, is it 'Barrow Bridge' or 'Barrowbridge'? Take your pick. In *Moorlands and Memories* Clarke hedges his bets and uses both versions. Today, most people settle with 'Barrow Bridge' so I'm going to go with the flow.

The 'Deserted Village'

However you spell it, it's still a lovely place. It was special to Allen Clarke and generations of Boltonians, myself included. The narrow road running up alongside the cottages, with the Dean Brook alongside, interspersed with traditional gas lamps, is a delight in any season. Its history is fascinating.

It developed in the late 18th century, with some workers' houses built alongside a mill, expanding as the industrial revolution gathered pace. The owners developed Barrow Bridge as a 'model village' with its own institute, school and facilities far better than most Bolton mill workers in the nearby town could even dream of. It was visited by Prince Albert and Disraeli was impressed by its achievements as a model of 'responsible capitalism'. Yet it all went sadly wrong. The mill closed as early as 1863, re-opened for a few years then shut down for good. Attempts were made to revive it, but failed. The fine stone cottages fell into decay with just a handful of tenants remaining. The institute became derelict.[47]

By the time Clarke was a young boy in Bolton in the 1870s it had become a 'deserted village'. He describes himself and friends playing the empty houses, perhaps with a sense of excitement and fear at the sight if the huge empty mill. As a young man starting to make his way as a writer, he developed his thoughts about

---

[46] *Moorlands* p.132

[47] See D. Billington and C. Walsh *Barrow Bridge* also Denis O'Connor *Barrow Bridge, Bolton, Dean Mills Estate: A Victorian Achievement*, Bolton 1982

the village. His first wife, who died so suddenly within months of their wedding, was brought up in the village. In 1893 he published *Tales of a Deserted Village* featuring some characters based on people he had known – in a series of short stories. One of those was extended into a novel and serialised in his *Northern Weekly* during 1898. *Summer-Storm: a woman and the consequence* was never published in book form.

Some of the stories were re-printed in his newspaper, *Teddy Ashton's Northern Weekly*. One tale features the visit of Prince Albert, who is introduced to the culinary delights of Lancashire potato cakes by one of the Barrow Bridge ladies.

As Clarke's network grew, he organised picnics and cycle rides to Barrow Bridge and other local beauty spots. But Barrow Bridge had pride of place. The culmination of this was the enormous 'Teddy Ashton Picnic' held on May 11th 1901, which is covered in detail in the next chapter. This was more than just a social gathering to promote his newspaper. The event was a fundraiser in aid of the locked-out quarrymen of Bethesda.

As well as 'The Great Picnic' of 1901 Clarke organised smaller visits to Barrow Bridge for his walking and cycling networks, including an outing of the Blackpool 'Speedwell Cycling Club' in the 1920s.

Barrow Bridge becomes Bolton's top tourist resort

Barrow Bridge started to revive, largely thanks to Clarke's efforts. He once ruefully commented that he had been thinking of buying a house there but prices had got too high for him to afford! By the 1930s, the village was flourishing. Local residents developed a tradition of making a bit of extra cash by offering refreshments to visitors. The former mill lodge was converted into a boating lake. The attractive village was within walking distance of places like Halliwell and Astley Bridge and was served by local buses. My own no. 4 bus from Green Lane along Crescent Road to Bolton town centre used to continue to the enticing and slightly romantic-sounding 'Barrow Bridge', making me regret having to get off at Trinity Church.

The 'Sixty-Three Steps' was a popular place for local visitors to have their photographs taken. The steps were provided for mill workers to get to work from the surrounding moorland cottages and 'folds', as well as enabling miners to get up to the Burnt Edge pits.

In the 20th century, the village became a victim of its own success. The 'boating lake', beloved by generations of children, was filled in. In its place there's now a car park. It's much quieter than it was back in the 1960s, there are no shops selling you lemonade or home-baked cakes, no children's swings. It's less special, though it's still a beautiful place. All the houses, and the former institute, are occupied and fetch much higher prices than Allen Clarke baulked at. Little remains of the mill, which was demolished before the First World War, leaving only the bell tower to survive until 1934. The coping stone from the bell-tower is in the middle of the bus turning circle.

When Clarke wrote *Moorlands and Memories* Moss Bank was still private, with the house and grounds out of bounds to the public. He hints that change was afoot, commenting at the end of his 'Barrow Bridge' chapter:

"..and what next? Perhaps a glorious park for Bolton. Let us hope so." [48]

His hopes were realised. Moss Bank Park is there for all to enjoy, though sadly the old house has gone and the miniature railway isn't operating. I hope that the railway, like its bigger counter-parts, will see its own revival.

Walking back to St Peter's

As you've probably realised by now, Clarke's book meandered around, criss-crossed on itself and sometimes visited favourite places more than once. I can be permitted to do a bit of the same. Clarke's favourite route, on foot, to Barrow Bridge was along Church Road. He comments on the St Peter's Church, 'the cathedral of Halliwell', which still graces Church Road. He describes the grave-yard as *"as bonny a place in which to rest when one's day is done, in this planet of pilgrimages and parting."*

Many eminent Boltonians are buried here, including W.F. Tillotson, founder of *The Bolton Evening News* and once Clarke's employer. Close to the church, up 'Captain's Clough' stood what Clarke refers to as 'Dobson's Hall', the home of Sir Benjamin Dobson, though the house was actually called 'Doffcockers'. It was demolished in 1913. It had its own miniature railway (they crop up everywhere if you look) which lay derelict for many years after the hall had been abandoned.

A very pleasant walk taking you back towards the town centre is along the linked footpaths through Captain's Clough. The walk is a delight at any time of year, but in mid-May, when the wild garlic and bluebells are at their most abundant best, it is breathtaking. The walk brings you out near Brownlow Fold. If you continue to meander through the side streets and past the old Halliwell Library, you'll get to Mere Hall. The fine building is now used by Bolton Music Service and other groups including the Registry Office.

---

[48] *Moorlands* p.136

Spring in Captain's Clough, with wild garlic in profusion

If you walk along Gaskell Street, past what remains of Nelson Mills and the small terrace of stone cottages, you get to where 'The Ginnel' used to be – Clarke remembers it as "*a fearsome lonely place*", reputedly haunted by those scary Lancashire creatures, boggarts. It was a link onto to Chorley Old Road. Sadly, it is now gated and locked, so any surviving boggarts have nobody to terrorise.

9. The Great Picnic: From Bolton to Bethesda

"....the daylight is dying over the mountains and the sunset is fair on bonny Bethesda – bonny Bethesda where babes want for bread. As I write, I see before me once again the faces in the mass meeting, the earnest, honest, resolved face, and the vast throng stands up and sings, fervently and pathetically, in Welsh, 'Land of My Fathers'.[49]

Clarke's finest hour? A unique example of children's solidarity

The active involvement of children in popular politics has been little-researched. One of the most remarkable examples occurred in the early years of the 20th century, during the long and bitter Penrhyn Lock-Out, in North Wales. Allen Clarke, through his 'Children's Column' in *Northern Weekly*, played the key role in galvanising a unique campaign, mobilising hundreds of Lancashire boys and girls to help their sisters and brothers in Wales.[50]

Barrow Bridge was at the heart of the campaign, as the location for Clarke's biggest-ever event – 'The Teddy Ashton Picnic' - organised to raise funds for the locked-out quarry workers. At a time when children and young people are becoming active in fighting climate change, recalling earlier examples of children's engagement in radical causes is important. The story of Lancashire children's support for their sisters and brothers in Wales during the Penrhyn Lock-Out has been hidden from history; it should be celebrated.

Britain's longest and most bitter industrial dispute

The enormous Penrhyn slate quarries at Bethesda in North Wales were the scene of what was one of the longest and most bitter struggles in British working class history. It began on November 22nd 1900 with the victimisation of a small group of quarrymen. It quickly spread to the entire quarry complex and became a fight for trade union rights, better working conditions and improved wages.[51]

Lord Penrhyn refused to even meet the men's representatives in the North Wales Quarrymen's Union, and kept them locked out for three years. Of the 2,800 men

---

[49] Allen Clarke in *Teddy Ashton's Northern Weekly* May 31st 1902

[50] This essay was first published in *Bolton People's History* in 1984 as *Feed My Lambs: Bolton Kids and the Penrhyn Lock-Out.* It has been updated with some additional information added.

[51] For a full account of the lock-out and the wider political and social context, see R. Merfyn Jones *The North Wales Quarrymen 1874-1922,* Cardiff, 1982

who came out, over a thousand never returned. The village of Bethesda was decimated – shops closed down, houses became empty and families were split up.

Although the men were ultimately defeated, Lord Penrhyn paid a high price. Never again did his quarries achieve their previously unrivalled position in the world slate market.

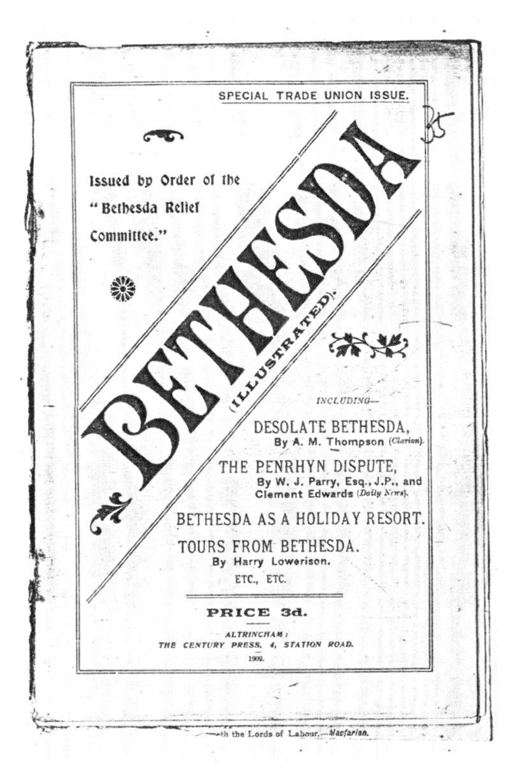

A pamphlet produced to win support for the locked-out Bethesda quarrymen

There was wide public sympathy for the men. What they were demanding was only what was enjoyed by workers in much of British industry, by the turn of the century. Popular daily papers like *The Morning Leader* and *Daily News* publicised the workers' case and raised money to ward off the creeping starvation that was looming over Bethesda. The union, and the Penrhyn Relief Committee, appealed for help to trades unionists and the public at large. The socialist movement did much to build support at a local level in many towns and cities across Britain.

Bolton to the fore

Perhaps nowhere was that support stronger than in Bolton. The local Labour Church, led by the veteran radical and friend of Clarke's, James Sims, played a key role in organising support.

The help that came from working class families, including children, was remarkable. It was the support from local children, many of whom were working in the mills as 'half-timers', which marked out Bolton's contribution as exceptional. [52]

Alongside the Labour Church, Allen Clarke and his newspaper *Teddy Ashton's Northern Weekly*, did much to galvanise support. It had a 'children's column' by Allen Clarke, writing as 'Grandad Grey', which encouraged young readers to

[52] The 'Half-Time System' forced working class children to work half-time in mills and factories and spend the rest of their day at school. It was prevalent in the textile districts of Lancashire and Yorkshire and was finally abolished in 1918. See Edmund and Ruth Frow *The Half Time System of Education*, Manchester 1970

contribute articles and poetry, and – as we shall see – get practically involved in the struggle.[53]

Local support grows

By the spring of 1901 it was clear that the Penrhyn Lock-Out would be a long and painful battle. Throughout Britain, trades unionists, socialists and other well-wishers were sending funds to help families in Bethesda. Bolton was at the forefront. One particular event helped to build local support to a high level. This was the great 'Teddy Ashton Picnic' held at the local beauty spot of Barrow Bridge, on May 11th 1901. He had begun planning the event some weeks earlier, promoting it through his *Northern Weekly*.

The great Barrow Bridge Picnic

Clarke had a ready-made audience for his picnic in aid of Bethesda, through his newspaper. He built up support for the event through local groups like the Labour Church and arranged special reduced rate tickets with the Lancashire and Yorkshire Railway. Wagonettes were on hand at Trinity Street station to take some of the visitors the three miles to Barrow Bridge, though most probably walked.

The picnic attracted a crowd of over 10,000, with people coming from all over Lancashire. There was entertainment provided by the local Clarion Choir and other musicians. The village institute laid on food to cater for the enormous crowds and quickly sold out. The village shop produced special 'Barrow Bridge Rock' which popular with the children. There was even a 'moving picture show' by local impresario Fenton Cross.

A posed photo of attendees at the Barrow Bridge Picnic, with a smartly-dressed Allen Clarke in the foreground standing on the right

---

[53] See *Lancashire's Romantic Radical: The Life and Work of Allen Clarke/Teddy Ashton*

The local constabulary had expressed concern to Clarke and the organisers that such a large crowd might cause disorder. In the event, a policeman turned up at Clarke's house the following day to thank him for a well-organised and entirely peaceful gathering! There wasn't a trace of litter.

Support from the unions

The trades unions of Bolton responded magnificently to the quarrymen's appeal. Nineteen unions in the town contributed money, with the powerful spinners' union contributing £150 and the Card and Blowing Room Operatives a further £150, with an additional £50 from the local branch. Individual branches, such as the Bolton Spinners' Atlas no. 1 Mill, contributed smaller amounts. Engineers, bleachers and dyers, carters, hairdressers, railwaymen, miners, printers and even life assurance agents sent in substantial sums.[54]

The choral concerts

In June 1901 the Bethesda Choir made their first visit to Bolton as part of a national fund-raising tour. They were back the following week, performing at a concert in the Temperance Hall organised by Bolton Trades Council and the local Co-operative Society. The officers of the Trades Council spoke, alongside by the president of Bolton Co-operative Society. They were followed by the Liberal MP George Harwood and Bolton socialist activist Fred Brocklehurst. James Sims did most of the promotion for the concert, selling tickets and organising publicity in conjunction with Clarke's *Northern Weekly*. The event was a great success and the choir were asked to come back for a further concert.

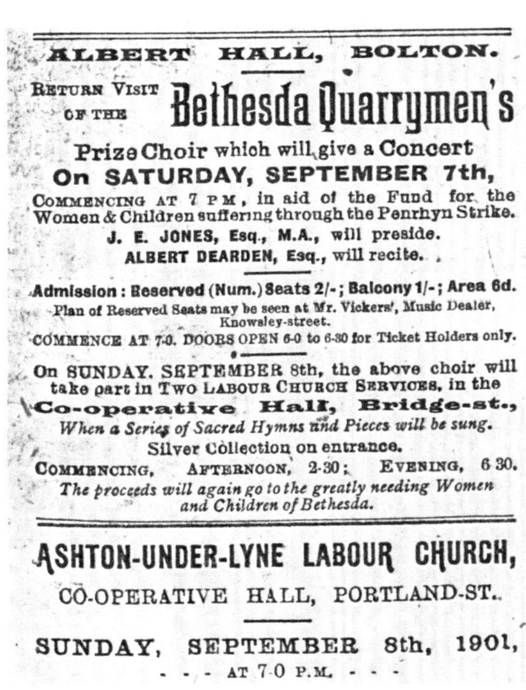
ALBERT HALL, BOLTON.
RETURN VISIT OF THE Bethesda Quarrymen's
Prize Choir which will give a Concert
On SATURDAY, SEPTEMBER 7th,
COMMENCING AT 7 P.M., in aid of the Fund for the Women & Children suffering through the Penrhyn Strike.
J. E. JONES, Esq., M.A., will preside.
ALBERT DEARDEN, Esq., will recite.
Admission: Reserved (Num.) Seats 2/-; Balcony 1/-; Area 6d.
Plan of Reserved Seats may be seen at Mr. Vickers', Music Dealer, Knowsley-street.
COMMENCE AT 7-0. DOORS OPEN 6-0 to 6-30 for Ticket Holders only.
On SUNDAY, SEPTEMBER 8th, the above choir will take part in TWO LABOUR CHURCH SERVICES, in the Co-operative Hall, Bridge-st.,
When a Series of Sacred Hymns and Pieces will be sung.
Silver Collection on entrance.
COMMENCING, AFTERNOON, 2-30; EVENING, 6 30.
The proceeds will again go to the greatly needing Women and Children of Bethesda.
ASHTON-UNDER-LYNE LABOUR CHURCH,
CO-OPERATIVE HALL, PORTLAND-ST.
SUNDAY, SEPTEMBER 8th, 1901,
AT 7-0 P.M.

An advert for the concert from *Teddy Ashton's Northern Weekly*

[54] The Hairdressers' Union contributed £21.10s. Other local donations included Gas Workers £3, Typographical Association £1, Wheelwrights £10, Atherton Miners £2, Wharton Hall Miners £2, Lostock Railwaymen £1, Saddlemakers £1, Carters £5, Tape Sizers £2 1s, Engine and Iron Grinders £2.

This time, the huge Albert Hall was the venue with reserved tickets selling for 2 shillings for the best seats down to sixpence. J. E. Jones, Headmaster of Bolton School, presided. A dialect recital was given by Albert Dearden. The following day, a Sunday, Bolton Labour Church put on two performances of the choir in the Co-operative Hall, at 2.30 and 6.00pm.

The concerts continued into 1902. By then, Bethesda possessed two male choirs and a ladies', which visited Bolton in November 1901. One of the male choirs came to Bolton for a weekend of concerts on February 1st and 2nd. The Albert Hall was the venue for the Saturday evening concert and the Temperance Hall hosted the Sunday performances. Both were organised by the Labour Church. Allen Clarke gave an account of the Albert Hall concert in *Northern Weekly*, commenting on a particularly fine rendition of 'Ash Grove'.

Barrow Bridge featured once again in the campaign, with a fund-raising concert held in the former Institute on Good Friday, 1902. The Harvey Street Choir, of Halliwell was conducted by Mr F. Hamer. Their performance was followed by readings from the work of Bolton dialect writer J. T. Staton (see Chapter 12). A report in *Northern Weekly* said that his comic tale, 'Soup for a Sick Mon', had the audience in tears of laughter.

The children join in

Following the February concert in the Albert Hall, Clarke hit on a novel idea to involve young readers of his paper. He ran a children's column in *Northern Weekly*, writing as 'Grandad Grey'. Some of the young readers of his column had parents who were socialist activists. Towns such as Bolton, Darwen and Burnley had a flourishing socialist culture, with active branches of the Independent Labour Party, Social Democratic Federation and Labour Church. There were 'Socialist Sunday Schools' which children attended and learned a socialism that was ethical, compassionate and inclusive. Clarke's *Northern Weekly* was a non-aligned labour/socialist paper which did much to popularise a distinctive 'Northern' socialism.[55]

At the beginning of February he published his first appeal, headed 'I WANT YOU TO HELP'. He gave a simple but moving account of the struggle so far, and asks:

"Now I want the children of England – and especially the children who read The Northern Weekly – to help the children of Bethesda. I want you to collect money for them. I want you to collect old clothes and shoes, and shirts, stockings etc., from your neighbours and friends; then we'll send the money and clothes to the

[55] See Paul Salveson *Walt Whitman and the Religion of Socialism in the North of England* (forthcoming, 2020/1)

poor children of Bethesda. For we must not let the big lord beat them and their families."

Northern Weekly] - - - - [*Collecting Card.*

"FEED MY LAMBS"

BETHESDA RELIEF FUND.

FROM THE CHILDREN OF ENGLAND TO THE CHILDREN OF BETHESDA.

[This money is being collected to help the starving children of the Bethesda quarrymen, who have, because of their trade-unionism, been locked out two years by Lord Penrhyn, and are still out.]

Name of Giver.	Address	Amount.
		£ s. d.
Sam Spinner	14, John St.	0 1 0
Mrs. Brown	28, James St.	2
Jos. Goodman	19, Elm St.	1
	Total £	

Collected by..................................

Address..................................

Town..................................

The children's collecting card, from *Teddy Ashton's Northern Weekly*

He showed an example of a collecting card which he had printed, *"filling in a few names to show you how to do it."*[56] The collecting card was headed 'FEED MY LAMBS - Bethesda Relief Fund' and was sub-titled 'From the children of England to the children of Bethesda'.

The card said *"This money is being collected to help the starving children of Bethesda quarrymen, who have because of their trade unionism been locked out for two years by Lord Penrhyn and are still out."*

The response was remarkable. Within a week 26 children had returned completed cards, with monies totalling £10.10.7. Most of the children were from the Bolton area, though others wrote in from Heywood, Ashton, Rochdale, Oldham and other Lancashire towns. Interest extended into the West Riding of Yorkshire, with children in Huddersfield and the Colne Valley involved in the collections.

Rachel Baxendale from Darwen replied to the appeal within two days:

"Dear Grandad, This is the first time in my life (that I have written a letter to a newspaper – ed.), but my dada said he would help me if I would try...We have read about the Bethesda children and we are sorry for those two little boys that had only one short for them both. We would like to help them if we could, and if you could please send us one of your collecting cards we will try. I may say that I am eight years old and in the second standard."

Yours truly, Rachel Baxendale"[57]

---

[56] *Northern Weekly* February 8th 1902

[57] *Northern Weekly* February 15th 1902

The following week, her contribution of 6s 5d was acknowledged in *The Northern Weekly*.

The money collected was sent on to the Rev. Lloyd, secretary of the Relief Committee. In his replies thanking the children for their great efforts he referred to the plight of some of the families:

"...a family of nine – father, mother and seven children. The father is in poor health and the mother has to keep some of the youngest children in bed to save their breakfasts. The Relief Fund cannot give more than 7s a fortnight on average."

Lloyd had a special message for the young readers of *Northern Weekly*:

"...our sincerest thanks to you on behalf of the Bethesda children for sympathising with them, who suffer through no fault of their own. They join their fathers and mothers in the processions of the workmen along the streets of our town carrying small banners and flags with Welsh inscriptions thereon, which translated mean 'It is better to die a soldier than live a traitor'. Thus they take part in one of the bitterest, longest labour struggles ever known, whose consequences in want and poverty are so appalling. Your subscriptions will cheer them up, I know, and will gladden the hearts of their parents."

Susie, Harold, Martha, Ezra and Lily

Susie Lord was a 13-year old girl working at Whitewell Slipper Works at Waterfoot in Rossendale.[58] She wrote to *The Northern Weekly* to say that a copy of the paper had been passed round the machine room and the girls decided to have a collection. It raised £1 15s 6d, and Susie became a regular contributor to the fund. The girls in the adjoining 'Turnshoe and Clicking Rooms' contributed a further 10s 6d.

Harold Hargreaves, of Barrowford, wrote in to say "*The weather is very nice for sliding, but I have given it up to go collecting for the children.*" Martha Smith, of Walkden, wrote to 'Grandad Grey' telling him "*I am sure Lord Penrhyn is not worthy of the name of man or he would not force little innocent children to starve and clem.*"

Ezra Brittan, age 11 of Oldham, said he was "*very sorry to think that children have to suffer through a bad man, even if he is a lord..if you ever come to Oldham, come to our house for tea – you will be welcome.*"

---

[58] The Rossendale Valley was noted for its footwear industry, particularly slipper manufacture. Large numbers of female labour, including half-timers such as Susie, were employed in the industry. It was highly unionised though I am not aware of whether children were admitted into the union.

One of the most touching letters published in *Northern Weekly* came from 'Lily', daughter of one of the locked-out quarrymen. It was headed 'A Letter from a Bethesda Child':

"Dear sir, I take this opportunity to thank you for your kindness, and to thank the children, who are collecting on behalf of the poor children at Bethesda, who have suffered so much during this cold weather. My father was at the mass meeting when Mr Lloyd read out some of the children's letters, and they were moved to tears when the sympathetic letters were read to the meeting. I am very glad to know you take so much interest in our cause, and that you intend to send an excursion here this summer, and I I would like to see some of the children when they come to Bethesda. We live on the top of a hill close to Bethesda, and my father is working at present in a slate quarry at the foot of Snowdon, and goes away early every Monday morning and comes back on Saturday, to spend the Sunday with us, and I don't like to part with him every Sunday night. I hope you will accept my sincere thanks, on behalf of the children, and that you will accept my mistakes, as I am a 9-year old Welsh girl, who does not know to write English properly. You may print this letter in a corner of your paper, if you think it is good enough.

Yours truly, Lily"[59]

FOR THE BETHESDA CHILDREN.

Collected by	£	s.	d.
Amount last week	21	8	4½
Joseph Heywood (Middleton).. ..	0	2	0
Jno. V. Windle (Burnley)	0	3	7½
Phœbe Clough (Cloughfold)	0	0	6
Ernest Duckworth (Bolton)	0	5	2
Polly Melling (Preston)	0	4	7
Helen Howard (Middleton) 2 cards ..	0	9	2
Harry Sutton (Weaste)	0	4	0
Ada Binns (Horwich) 2nd. card ..	0	3	10
Samuel Durham (Nelson)	0	9	0
Millicent Brown ,, 3 cards ..	1	3	1
L. Brown (Openshaw)	0	5	0
Willie Entwistle (Blackburn).. ..	0	4	0
Squire Knowles (Ashton-u-Lyne) ..	0	4	2
Willie Nickeas (Beswick) 2 cards ..	0	8	0
Edith Thornton (Huddersfield) ..	0	5	0
Maggie Hamer (Barrowford)	0	7	9
Bertha Smith (Whitefield)	0	2	0
Thos. E. Watkins (Barrow-in-Fur) ..	0	9	0
Lily May ,, ,, ..	0	7	[illegible]
Annie Pownall (Glossop)	0	6	2
J. W. Moss (Beswick)	0	4	1
E. A. ,, ,, ...	0	3	0
Herbert Thorpe (Horwich)	0	5	6
Robert Eachus (Manchester) 3rd card	0	4	2
Ada Bentley (Lees)	0	5	5
Winnie Plant (Bolton) 2nd card ..	0	3	6
Laura Pearson (Golcar)	0	4	3
Ernest Radcliffe (Nelson)	0	6	4
Subscribers:			
R. C. (Walsden)..	0	0	3
H. Cooper & family (Stoke Newington)	0	2	6
W. Crabtree (Derby)	0	1	6
E. F. F. (Pemberton)	0	0	9
"Lost Ends" (Rochdale)	0	5	0
Total	£29	17	8

A list of the collectors' contributions, published in *Northern Weekly,* February 22nd 1902

Holidays in Bethesda

The excursion which Lily refers to was part of one of the ideas to assist the quarrymen's families. Organisations such as local co-operative societies and *The Northern Weekly* arranged holidays to Bethesda, with accommodation provided in the quarrymen's cottages.

[59] *Northern Weekly* February 22nd 1902

At Whitsun 1902 Clarke organised a cycle trip from Bolton to Bethesda, offering 25s for full board for the week, or 5s for a day. The route was out via Chester and the coast, returning via an inland route through Betws-y-Coed and Wrexham. He extolled *"the cleanliness and sweet homeliness of the people"* and the fine mountain scenery, walks, fishing and fresh air.

He produced some of his most powerful journalism during his Bethesda visits. In a full page editorial in *The Northern Weekly* headed 'Where Babes Want for Bread', he contrasts the beauty of Snowdonia with the suffering taking place there:

"Beautiful are the mountains about Bethesda, beautiful are the vales and waters, beautiful the lanes and trees, beautiful the white lambkins on the green hillsides – but blighted are the homes of the workers in the midst of this because one man has hardened his heart, because one man selfishly holds a piece of Nature that neither he, nor his ancestors, ever made, and to which he has really no more sole right than the humblest drudge in this village of Bethesda, over which he is Lord till death reduces him to his deserved level."

The messianic Christian socialist tone continues to the end of the piece:

"I must finish now. As I cease the daylight is dying over the mountains and the sunset is fair on bonny Bethesda – bonny Bethesda where babes want for bread. As I write, I see before me once again the faces in the mass meeting, the earnest, honest, resolved face, and the vast throng stands up and sings, fervently and pathetically, in Welsh, 'Land of My Fathers'. And I say to myself, as the sunset lights end, and shadows fall across the garden in front of the cottage, and through the window upon my paper, 'May the glorious morning soon come, the morning of rejoicing for Bethesda!"[60]

The end

That morning never came. The lead story of *The Northern Weekly* for October 17th 1903 was headed 'A Long and Bitter Lock-out'. It was a valiant attempt to rally support for what was a dying cause. A few weeks later it was all over, with only a selected number of the men being allowed to return to work.

The children's fund raised £147 9s 5d. It was a small sum in comparison to the thousands raised by newspaper campaigns such as that mounted by the *Morning Leader* and the contributions from the big unions. But in many ways it is more remarkable. The children who contributed were from ordinary working families. Some of them were half-timers in local mills and factories. The letters of the young children, from ages of seven or eight, show an amazing degree of maturity and compassion.

---

[60] *Northern Weekly* May 31st 1902

Perhaps some of the children involved in the Bethesda appeal went on to become leaders in their communities, or in the socialist and trade union movement. We know little about them. Nor do we know if the friendships created during the lock-out, through the visits of the choirs to Lancashire and the excursions to Bethesda, resulted in continuing links between towns like Bolton and Bethesda. It would be good to think that they did.

Whitewell Slipper Works in the 1920s. Photo courtesy The Whitaker, Rawtenstall

10. Over Belmont and Darwen Moors

"The route I oftenest take to Belmont is Brian Hey...It is grand to walk or ride this way in the early morning on a summer's day, when the sun is dispelling the gauzy moorland mists, and the birds are piping in the sweet solitude."[61]

Belmont features often in *Moorlands and Memories*. It remains a delightful village, though plagued by traffic. In Clarke's day, it was his favourite cycling route from Bolton to Blackpool, despite being hillier than the alternative route along Chorley New Road through Horwich. The moors stretching across from Belmont to Darwen are some of our most beautiful and are full of history and folklore.

Boggarts over Belmont

Clarke takes us, on his bike, past what was The Wright's Arms (there's now a nice cafe and deli next to the Italian eatery, San Marino) and down into the dip before the start of the climb up the village street. He praises the purity of the water from the fountain, close to the Black Dog Inn. The pub was closed during my ride in May, but I'm glad to see it has re-opened.

Beyond the village Clarke introduces one of his favourite topics – *boggarts*. They are a special species of Lancashire hobgoblin, ghost or spirit. As we've already seen, on Gaskell Street, there are urban as well as rural types. Most Lancashire writers in Victorian times mentioned them, and some still do, I'm very glad to say. But they are in danger of extinction. It's about time someone set up a Boggart Preservation Society; I'm sure there would be grants available.

The Belmont boggart lived somewhere along the road outside the village, before the track off to Bromiley's Farm. It's near to the bus terminus, though I doubt that boggarts would be allowed on board today's 535, with or without a mask, even if they had a concessionary bus pass. Clarke writes:

"There is said to be a boggart or ghost on this road – somewhere between this farm and the village. Not ever having been on this road in the dark, I cannot vouch for the spectre myself, but tradition tells that a great many years ago, early in the nineteenth century, or the later part of the eighteenth, a young man, after being executed for robbing a coach was found to be innocent, and the legend says that he haunts this spot, calling out to such persons as pass that way at night, 'Do you believe me innocent?' and must continue at that uncanny job till some unscared soul kindly answers, 'Yes'. Wherefore, I entreat you, for pity's sake, if you ever

---

[61] *Moorlands* p.138

come across this poor ghost...to reply to his plaintive query in the affirmative." [62]

Hopefully someone has taken up Clarke's request. I'm not aware of any boggart-sightings in recent times. Bromiley's is a historic place. The late editor of *The Chorley Guardian*, George Birtill, suggests that it was once occupied by two Huguenot refugees who wove there. However, he puts forward an even more interesting theory that the two brothers who lived there in the late 17th century were 'Hutterities' from Moravia. The original buildings have a semi-ecclesiastical appearance suggesting a Moravian influence.[63]

Looking across to Belmont and 'The Island' from Longworth Moor

Teddy Ashton's Well

Clarke was a great self-publicist and one of his most well-known bits of self-promotion lies further along Belmont Road, towards Abbey Village. This is 'Teddy Ashton's Well', which he christened after himself, with characteristic lack of modesty, sometime before or during the First World War. It is actually called 'Slate Well' and is opposite Lower Roddlesworth Farm. It's dangerous to stop a car there, so don't try. However, cyclists can use it for the purpose which Clarke intended, as a nice comfortable spot to sample some clean moorland water, prior to tackling the last climb towards Belmont. But you'd need take the back road to the farm and ask permission. He describes its products as *"the most felicitous unfuddling liquor in the world. Dame Nature's choicest brew."* [64]

The comment highlights a facet of Clarke's character – his disinterest in alcohol. It

---

[62] *Moorlands* pp.144-5

[63] George Birtill *Heather in My Hat*, Chorley 1977, p.27

[64] *Moorlands* p.147

was common in the 1890s and 1900s for socialists and liberals to be 'tee-total' owing to the effects of drink on working class families. Bolton Socialist Club, in its early years, had a 'no alcohol' rule. On a personal level, Clarke may have avoided drink because his father was over-fond of a pint. Throughout *Moorlands and Memories*, and indeed *Windmill Land*, you'll find few references to pubs. Those which do feature are mostly there for historical reasons and not, generally, as recommended stopping-off points.

Back in 1986 a few of us, including bookseller George Kelsall, Denis and Wendy Pye, veteran cyclist Albert Winstanley and Bolton's chief librarian Norman Parker, re-dedicated the well to 'Teddy Ashton', as our own piece of self-promotion to launch the new edition of *Moorlands and Memories*. It seems to have gone back to its overgrown state by now.

'Teddy Ashton's Well' - the 1986 event to launch re-publication of *Moorlands and Memories*

Hollinshead Hall and the 'Wishing Well'

Clarke mentions another nearby well that can be more easily visited. It is in the area around Hollinshead Hall – which was in ruins even in 1920. The farm, in front of the hall, was still working when Clarke visited, though today both buildings have gone, apart from some partly-demolished walls. However, the well house, which was next to the hall, remains. It's a remarkable place, probably dating from the late eighteenth century but the inside looks older. It can be accessed by foot or bike from the Tockholes Road, or from the main Belmont Road, off the area known as 'Piccadilly'. Clarke refers to it as a 'wishing well' and members of his walking party (below) took advantage of its miraculous properties before setting off over the indistinct track to Great Hill.

They passed what is today a house on the main road which Clarke tells us was once a pub – The Dog and Moor Game – opposite where the path leaves the road. It's a much easier path to tread these days. Look out for the ruins of old farmhouses as you ascend Great Hill – old Pimm's is on the right by a clump of trees. Just west of Great Hill are the ruins of Great Hill Farm, sheltering in the lea of the hill. I had an interesting encounter with a sheep there, 'playing dead' (the sheep, not me). It had got itself stuck in a gully and was lying on its back. After a lot of effort on my part the sheep roused itself and returned to its mates, without a word of thanks. That's sheep for you.

A 'rail ramble' from Darwen to Chorley

In *Moorlands and Memories* he describes a family 'rail ramble' organised by Bolton Labour Church's Sunday Afternoon Class in 1904, from Darwen to Chorley:

"There were youngsters with us on this long walk, and they footed it famously. Two little girls from Darwen did champion; also a little boy from the same place. The father of the girls told us that at the 'Northern Weekly' Barrow Bridge picnic they walked all the way from Darwen and back (about 20 miles)." [65]

The Bolton contingent took the train to Darwen alighting at what was then a substantial station with a large complement of staff. The party would have walked down past the fine Carnegie Library and adjacent art school, by the market hall to 'The Circus'.

In those days Darwen had its own local authority and the corporation operated a busy tram network, being one of the first in the world to use steam trams, from its opening in 1879. Two of the fine, almost palatial, waiting rooms are today used as shops at The Circus. There's a memorial at the former 'reversing triangle' half-way up Bull Hill next to 'The Tramway Cafe' whose owner Becky Johnson's great-great uncle worked on the trams. Darwen also had its own Literary Society; a very cultured place.

Today the town is subsumed under its larger neighbour, as part of 'Blackburn with Darwen Council'. Why do we have to have this obsession with centralisation, letting towns lose their identities and with it much of their pride? Perhaps one day we'll go back to smaller units of local government. 'Big' isn't always better.

The walking group met some friends from the local socialist movement before

---

[65] *Moorlands* p.170

carrying on through Bold Venture Park, passing India Mill with its enormous and highly-ornate chimney. They walked up to Jubilee Tower, which had not long been built, admiring the views across to the Irish Sea.

Freeing of the moors

The walk would not have been possible a few years earlier when parts of Darwen Moor were closed off by the landowners, the Duckworth family. In September 1896, the same month that the Winter Hill issue erupted, the people of Darwen won their right to roam. William Thomas Ashton and his sons led the campaign and won a hard-fought legal battle which took place over many years. Finally, the 'lord of the manor, Rev. A.W. Duckworth conceded defeat.

The people's victory was celebrated by a procession to the top, on Saturday September 5th 1896, the same weekend as the epic Winter Hill demonstration, which took place on the Sunday. The local socialists were prominent in the Darwen celebrations, and I imagine some of them joined the Bolton ramblers on their walk that summer's day in 1904.

The official opening of Darwen Tower, September 22nd 1898. *Photo courtesy of Harold Heys*

Jubilee Tower, ostensibly erected to mark Queen Victoria's golden jubilee, was also built to celebrate the freeing of the moors for all. *The Darwen News* observed that the tower would be..."*a landmark to be seen far and wide and, whilst, commemorating the record year, it would also fulfil a similar function with regard to the Freedom of the Darwen Moor.*"[66]

---

[66] In Harold Heys 'The Tower watches over thousands of acres of 'free' land'

The official celebration of the opening of the tower took place on September 22nd 1898, with a crowd estimated at over three thousand.[67]

The tower has stood guard over the people's rights of access to the moors ever since, though it came close to demolition in the early 1970s as a result of neglect and the ferocious weather it had withstood for decades. Fortunately, through the efforts of Councillor Bill Lees, a local GP, the tower was saved. It's an ongoing battle to maintain the tower and more recently (see below) there was a campaign to raise funds for its upkeep. [68]

Owd Aggies and Tockholes

The Bolton and Darwen comrades would have dropped down from the tower past 'Owd Aggie's' – a famous local landmark which featured in a dramatic event one night in November 1860 when three local louts broke in and attacked the old couple – 'Aggie' and her husband John. They got away with some cash but were quickly tracked down and arrested. Local legend had it that the couple were murdered in their bed but Aggie lived to testify against the robbers and died of old age in 1862.

The story goes that 'Owd Aggie's' made her own sarsaparilla for mill workers walking over to the mills at Darwen. In later years the house became a popular tea room for thirsty ramblers making their way up to the tower. Owd Aggies was demolished many years ago but there's a very good cafe nearby – Vaughns at Ryal Fold, Tockholes, next to The Royal pub.

An early 20th century view of 'Owd Aggies'. *Courtesy Harold Heys*

---

67 I am grateful to notes supplied by Harold Heys and Tony Greenwood on the fight for access to Darwen moors and to Harold Heys for information on 'Owd Aggie's'.
68 See Harold Heys, above

Clarke was fond of Tockholes and wrote about one of one of its illustrious sons, John Osbaldeston (1780 – 1862), inventor of the 'weft fork'. Like his Bolton fellow-inventor Samuel Crompton, he got very little for his efforts which helped to revolutionise the weaving process. He is buried in Tockholes churchyard. Before his death he wrote his own epitaph:

"Here lies John Osbaldeston, a humble inventor who raised many to wealth and fortune, but himself lived in poverty and died in obscurity – the dupe of false friends and the victim of misplaced confidence."[69]

Adding insult to injury, he didn't get the epitaph he had specified, but Clarke suggests *"he now sleeps serenely enough in the little churchyard amid the great green solitude of the moors, where the skylarks sing in the pink of the year, and the pewits make their plaintive cry."*[70]

Fine views, modest memorials and ruins

Let's return to that Labour Church ramble of 1904 that Clarke took us on. The party picnicked at Hollinshead Hall, some 'made wishes' in the well house and then a few members of the group headed back to Bolton, on foot. Others were determined to make it to Chorley, across Withnell Moor. Apparently the going was quite difficult from Belmont Road to Great Hill, but they made it.

The walk took them past Drinkwater's Farm, now a ruin, where they were given milk by the farmer's wife. Most of the farms in this area were bought by Liverpool Corporation after the Second World War as part of their water supply scheme and were demolished. Remains of Pimm's, Great Hill Farm and Drinkwater's can still be seen.

Drinkwater's today, looking up to Great Hill

---

69 Quoted in *Moorlands* p.162

70 *Moorlands* p.163

The path from Hollinshead Hall up to Great Hill is in better condition today than it seemed to be when Clarke's group walked it. And there is a fine viewing point at the summit, looking out across the West Lancashire Plain and on to Southport and over towards Pendle.

Drinkwater's is a special place, having a slightly eerie feel to it. Look out for 'Joe's Cup' – a modest and fitting memorial for Joe Whitter, a fell runner who died in 1991 at the age of 52. He asked for his ashes to be scattered here, a place he loved and often used as part of his circuit. There is a small plaque fixed onto a rock by a spring, with the cup usually lying behind. In 'normal' times there is an annual 'Joe's Cup Hill Race', but it was postponed this year. When I looked for it in June the cup had gone, but hopefully this was a precaution due to the coronavirus scare. Let's hope it is replaced and the race is revived next year.

Looking south from Drinkwater's is Round Loaf, an ancient burial chamber which has been excavated in recent decades. There is a path but it can be difficult after heavy rain. If you keep going beyond Round Loaf you'll come out in Lead Mines Clough, taking you to Anglezarke.

Clarke's group would have continued past Drinkwater's and by the remains of the mines which are still visible on the left. Soon after, the path splits with one track heading off towards Withnell. One of the sturdy 'Peak and Northern' signs directs you either to Withnell or White Coppice. Go left, downhill towards White Coppice. The badly-eroded path takes you out by the cricket ground, where – at least in normal times – teas and light snacks are available in the pavilion. It must be one of the loveliest locations for a cricket ground anywhere in the country.

The track takes you down past the school and to the small group of houses which make up the hamlet of White Coppice. One of the most celebrated residents was W.E. Eccles, a religious devotee of the old school, but a man who did a lot of good for his community, including the establishment of a small co-operative shop. Clarke mentions the 'tiny mission church' that was Eccles' HQ.

From there, Allen Clarke's group headed along *"pleasant winding lanes, where lovers wandered under the bright stars – the wooded hill called The Nab, looking like a dark thick cloud on our left – we made our way through the locality curiously christened Botany Bay, to Chorley, whose town hall was our guiding light for miles. From Chorley we took train home, healthily tired with our long moorland ramble..."* [71]

---

[71] *Moorlands* p.171

Up there today

It's sad that so many of the farms are now just ruins. But Darwen Tower remains, and you can (if you're brave enough to battle the winds) go to the top. It's well worth it, especially on a clear day. However, the tower is once again in need of a bit of fettling. A public subscription has been launched to raise funds for its restoration and at the time of writing £75,000 has been raised. Darwen Rotary is leading the fundraising effort.

Darwen Tower

11. Longworth Clough: two rides in times of crisis, a century apart

"...Nature is serenely wise. She takes no count of men's guilt, of human woes. She proceeds with her pretty business of the pageant of the seasons, whatever happens. The birds sing and the flowers bloom, and the sun shines in Longworth Clough, as if there has never been a murder there."[72]

One of Clarke's favourite bike rides out of Bolton was to go up through Dunscar to Egerton and then down Longworth Road, over towards Belmont. He describes a summer's bike ride with his wife and cycling companion:

"It is sweet and bonny in Longworth Clough on a summer's day – say such a day as the June afternoon when My Lady and I rode along the moorland road on the rim of the Clough from Egerton to Belmont. You go along the row of stone houses, then down the descent that was once a bridge across a fair little glen, there is a momentary glimpse of Belmont Church three miles in front of you...skylarks and throstles are singing, the voice of the cuckoo is head about the trees up the valley, the sward is decked with buttercups and daisies, and dandelion, and here and there a clump of gorse makes golden flame by the roadside." [73]

Although Clarke describes a seemingly idyllic scene, he goes on to refer to a much darker episode in the clough's history. In November 1889 it was the scene of the horrific murder of a young schoolteacher from Dunscar, Elizabeth Ann Holt. She taught at the school in Belmont and set off each Monday, on foot, to her work. She lodged in the village and returned home on Fridays. Whilst on her way Belmont, on a misty morning, she had her throat cut by a local man, James Macdonald, whose advances had been rejected. The body was found five days later; the murderer was arrested and confessed his guilt. Her funeral, at Walmsley Church, was attended by 15,000 people; she was buried in the family grave.

Clarke speculates on how a place can have an 'atmosphere', referring to a line of trees on the hillside, close to the scene of the murder. *"When I first saw them there was a sort of uncanny fascination about those gaunt trees – they suggested witchcraft, deeds of darkness, crime."*[74]

He revisits the scene with his friend whom he describes as 'The Occult Student' to visit the scene of the horror. Despite the man's horrendous act, Clarke comments

---

[72] *Moorlands* p.195

[73] *Moorlands* p.193

[74] *Moorlands* p.194

that his friend is against capital punishment, observing that "*most murderers are insane...and ought not to be executed, but kept in confinement and medically treated till restored to reason and righteousness*." That enlightened view was certainly not common at the time, and Macdonald was hanged for his crime.

Clarke quotes a poem written about the crime by his friend Wilfred Cryer, of Farnworth. It begins:

> *"Dismally dawned the fatal day!*
> *Misty and sombre-hued;*
> *When thou, dear form, were torn away*
> *To death and solitude;*
> *To a ravine, whose tragic scene*
> *With horror deep was viewed!"*[75]

Clarke was fascinated by the crime, which sent shock waves across Lancashire at the time. He wrote a novel, serialised in his *Northern Weekly* and later re-published in *Liverpool Weekly Post,* called 'A Gallows Soul – Murder in the Clough'.[76]

Clarke puts thoughts of murder and retribution behind him, as he and his wife continue their cycle ride along the road towards Belmont, "*in the distance, Belmont Church again, and behind all, the background of the view, the dark ridge, long and high, of Winter Hill*."[77]

Looking down to the village of Belmont from the Rivington road; Ward's Reservoir, or 'The Blue Lagoon', ahead

[75] *Lays After Labour*, Wilfred Cryer, Bolton 1902

[76] It was serialised in *Northern Weekly*, from November 26th 1904. It was again serialised in *Liverpool Weekly Post* from September 26th to November 19th, 1910, as 'Murder in the Clough'.

[77] *Moorlands* p.194

Clarke mentions the option of going down the lane which leads to the bleachworks, passing through the works yard, then up to the main road by 'the little stone school'. The Clarkes wisely decided to continue along the road which leads to the reservoir, bringing you out at the top end of the village.

I followed the same route on a chilly day in late March, as The Lockdown had begun in earnest. I was taking my 'permitted' exercise. Clarke was writing during the First World War, escaping news of the carnage by exploring the surrounding countryside. Even at the height of the First World War, there were probably fewer restrictions on people's movements than in Britain in 2020. A pleasant diversion took me past Walmsley's historic Unitarian chapel, currently locked-down but hoping to re-open with its Friday morning cafe soon.

Its website tells us: "*Walmsley Unitarians share the values of mutual respect and care for each other with an attitude which is down to earth, humorous, warm and friendly. Here, a sense of spiritual community and belonging is valued through building connections by meeting together. People hold a variety of religious/spiritual beliefs and approaches, alongside the basic Unitarian tenet of respect for the inherent worth and dignity of all beings.*"

It adds "*We are all divine sparks of the greater Light of the spirit. In our meditations, may we envision ourselves filled with this light and feel its potential healing power within. And may our communities and all beings on our planet earth be held in the light that is Love.*"

Billy Button and Eagley

My route took me via Astley Bridge and Bromley Cross, through Eagley Bank where Clarke's friend R.H. Brodie ('Billy Button') lived in the early years of the 20th century at 4 Ollerton Street. He was the first secretary of the Lancashire Authors' Association, of which Clarke was its first and less than effective chair. Brodie himself was a talented and often quite radical writer who deserves more recognition. He wrote regularly for *Teddy Ashton's Northern Weekly*. One of his dialect sketches, published in the April 21st 1906 edition, is an anti-war dialect sketch called 'Th'Invasion Bogey'. He published several collections of poetry, including *Random Rhymes.* He had many dialect sketches published in *The Bolton Journal* and *Liverpool Weekly Post*. One of his most well-known poems was 'A Lay o'Lancashire', part of which reads:

> *"There's mony a humble weiver*
> *Workin' fro' morn till neet*
> *Con donce wi' ony maiden*
> *Yo'll come across i'th'street*

Wi' her breakfast can an' basket,
Yo'll see her skip along,
An' when her looms get swingin'
Hoo'll sing a lively song." [78]

If on foot or bike you can continue through the fascinating industrial village of Eagley Bank and head down the cobbled lane to Eagley Bottoms. Clarke mentions Brodie telling him that the millworkers would take off their shoes (or more likely, clogs) during winter and walk down the cobbles in their stockinged feet to get the huge mill complex in the valley bottom. Today, some of the mills have survived, converted into attractive apartments.

Further up the hill I pass The Spread Eagle pub, with a long, carefully-spaced queue of people outside, waiting for provisions in the 'community market' created in the bar. It's good to hear that the pub has been nominated for an award for its role during the coronavirus emergency. I hope they win!

The climb up Hough Lane stiffens though my electric motor provides useful assistance. At the top I turn left and head towards Dunscar and the memorial to those killed in the conflict which Clarke was living through when he was writing. Perhaps in years to come there will be new memorials, to those who have died in the coronavirus episode.

I turn right at the junction and climb up through Egerton village. There's little traffic on the roads. Down to the left are the attractive cottages that make up Egerton Fold, where Clarke tells us that the master cotton-spinner, Horrocks, was born. At Longworth Road I take the left turn which Clarke described, passing the stone houses and across the clough, still looking looking very pretty. Belmont Church is visible in the distance. The road climbs gently, past Delph Sailing Club – closed for the duration of the pandemic – on the right.

Old industries

The remains of a paper mill are on the left, across the valley. The former - bleachworks is now a 'mixed use' of small businesses including a cycle shop. I hope they are managing to survive these troubled times (a lot of bike shops have prospered!). Winter Hill is still there, exuding its brooding presence. The masts wouldn't have been there in Clarke's day and perhaps he wouldn't have approved. But they are so much a part of the Winter Hill landscape it would be hard to imagine the view without them. Like Clarke, I avoid the steep road down past the old bleachworks and carry on towards the reservoir. This section of road has the

---

[78] In J. Randal Swann (ed.) *Lancashire Authors*, St Annes, 1924, p.53

advantage of being a 'dead end' for cars, with a gate when you reach the reservoir - but there's room for a bike to get through. Belmont village is stretched out down the hill to my left, with the waters of Belmont Reservoir ahead. I like it here. I reach the main road and turn back down the hill through Belmont. It's now a prosperous 'commuter village' with the small workers' cottages having been made into attractive homes.

A 1980s view of Belmont Bleachworks

There is a memorial – 'the water monument' - to the village's efforts to ensure its water supply was protected when Bolton created Belmont Reservoir to supply the growing conurbation. It was erected in 1907 by Edward Deakin, mill owner and patron of the local St Peter's church, to commemorate a clause in the Bolton Corporation Act of 1905 to protect the flow of water into Eagley Brook from Belmont Reservoir. Eagley Brook, along with water from the 'Blue Lagoon', provided an essential water supply to the bleaching and dyeing works and there was a danger that taking too much water from Belmont Reservoir to supply Bolton's homes and businesses would have a detrimental effect on the bleach works. The clause on the monument states that as compensation for taking water for Bolton the Corporation had to ensure a continuous flow down Eagley Brook "*between 5am and 5pm every day except Sunday, Good Friday and Christmas Day*." Clarke was unimpressed, commenting that it was a rather dull-looking inscription.

Belmont still has a pub, The Black Dog, normally a very welcome stopping-off point. The virus has put paid to any thought of a lunch-time pint so I carry on. The other pub that I can remember, The Bull, is being converted into a private house.

By The Black Dog is the junction with the steeply-graded road over to Rivington, by the ever-popular 'Blue Lagoon', or 'Ward's Reservoir'. When I was younger I used to see it as a challenge to get up to the summit without having to stop, or – still worse – get off and walk. I always made it. I couldn't do that on a normal bike these days, though my electric bike gets me up with relatively little effort. And the view from the top is as stunning as ever.

Today, I'm heading back towards Bolton, past the former bleachworks and new houses on the left, then up the hill by the deli and restaurant that was once The Wright's Arms. The former pub featured prominently in the Winter Hill events of 1896. It was the 'end point' for the thousands of walkers who had asserted their right of way over the hill. Whether the landlord was prepared for the huge throng we don't know but he ran out of beer! It did pretty well when we organised the first commemoration, in 1982. Like everywhere else at the time of my ride, the cafe and restaurant were closed 'for the duration'. Thankfully, both have reopened.

It's an easy and attractive ride back towards Bolton, with fine views across to Egerton on the left, beyond Springs Reservoir. There's the magnificent classical 'frieze' on the right, below the Waterworks Cottage built in 1824. On the front gable end there's a relief plaque showing a seated female figure pouring water into a vessel held by a child, the design is echoed by a larger plaque on the road below.

Whimberry Hill, over to the right, is fascinating and a bit mysterious. There are no footpaths shown on the map but there are some informal routes. The area had a number of small coal pits and I can remember in the early 1980s coming across some ancient tramway track suspended above a clough. The area is explored in *Winter Hill and Anglezarke Scrapbook* by Messrs. Lane, Cartwright and Rhodes. They make the dry comment that the one form of vegetation that doesn't exist on the hill is the tasty whimberry. Vast expanses of heather are a good substitute.

Soon after Waterworks Cottage the road to Walker Fold veers off to the right, with a sharp climb through the stone quarries, which Clarke often mentions in *Moorlands and Memories*. It's a long while since Wilton Quarry was worked but today the remains present a spectacular sight. At the top of the climb it's worth stopping to admire the view across Bolton towards Manchester. The lack of car traffic this Spring has meant that the skies are much clearer and you can see across to the Peak District and Wales.

Clarke's favourite bike route from Bolton to Preston was this way, over Belmont. Returning, he'd take this road by the quarries, along Scout Road and then down

Longshaw Ford Road to Barrow Bridge. It's the same route I take, keeping a careful control on the brakes dropping down the steep single track road that brings you out into one of Bolton's prettiest places. But that's a story for an earlier chapter. Repetitive? Me?

The Bolton Waterworks – the 'classical' frieze on Belmont Road

12. Staton, Teddy Ashton and Tum Fowt

"Tum Fowt is a very little hamlet (it's noan Shakespeare's Hamlet mind yo') abeaut a mile east o'Trotterteawn, or Bowton, an' lies between t'latter place an' Bury, just off th'heigh road. Th'River Tonge crawls close by, an' there's a cemetery a toothri yards off, wheer a lot o'deead folk lives."[79]

Let's get the bus out to Tum Fowt, or Tonge Fold as it is shown on google, and have a look around. It's the place that Clarke immortalised in his *Tum Fowt Sketches*, of which he claimed to have sold over a million copies in newsagents, station bookstalls and through his own shops in Blackpool and Bolton.

J.T. Staton, Tum Fowter and Journalist

It wasn't Clarke who turned Tum Fowt into a literary shrine. That honour must go to an earlier writer, J.T. Staton, who was also responsible for the name of my little publishing operation, *Lancashire Loominary*.

Clarke admits of Tonge Fold that *"the dialect version of its name, 'Tum Fowt', was first given some celebrity by a Bolton editor and author, J.T. Station, who, as is fitting, is buried in the adjacent cemetery."* [80] Clarke admired Staton and his writing and shared his slightly surreal sense of humour. He knew his son, with whom he played billiards.

Staton was born in Bolton, on Bradshawgate in 1817 but was orphaned at an early age and attended Chetham's School in Manchester. He grew into a highly talented journalist, writing in both standard English and dialect. His magazine – *Th' Bowtun Loominary*, which later became *The Lankishire Loominary* - was almost entirely in dialect and was a mix of gossip, comment and tomfoolery. The title in full, although it varied on a regular basis, was *The Bowtun Loominary, Tum Fowt Telegraph un Lankishire Lookin Glass*.

Writing in *The Lancashire Annual*, R.H. Brodie said of him: *"J.T. Staton were left an orphan, an' he were brout up i'th' Chetham's College. He were th'fust editor o'th'Bowton Evening' News...Staton rendered greit service to Bowton, for th' Associated Burial Societies o'Bowton made him a present of a handsome writing' desk; an' he also translated for Prince Lucien Bonaparte 'Th'Song o'Solomon' into th' Bowton twang."* [81]

---

[79] Teddy Ashton (Allen Clarke) Preface to *Tum Fowt Sketches*, Bolton 1892

[80] *Moorlands* p.270

[81] 'Th' Bowton Loominary and its Author' by Billy Button, *Teddy Ashton's Lancashire Annual* 1923

He had a highly developed sense of humour that went with a strong edge of radicalism, expressed in often biting satire. The *Loominary*, in its various forms, appeared between 1852 and 1864. During its final years it struggled to maintain its audience owing to the privations of the Cotton Famine. Its pages have a lot of comment on the American civil war and Staton championed the anti-slavery cause.

Tum Fowt an' *Th'Bowtun Loominary*

Like many other writers of the period, Staton published a number of sketches as 'penny readings' using a typical Lancashire figure, 'Bobby Shuttle'. However, his character was a dying breed – one of the few remaining handloom-weavers who once formed the bedrock of Lancashire working class radicalism and culture. He uses the character to look at contemporary issues through the eyes of an old man.

In the 1870s, when he was working as a journalist on *The Bolton Evening News* and *Farnworth Observer*, Staton published several readings including 'Bobby Shuttle wi'th'Demonstrationists' (1874). The story was about Bobby Shuttle getting the train from Moses Gate into Manchester to join the great trades union demonstration in support of the agricultural workers' strike. After joining 'a collier from Little Lever' at the station he sets off to Salford.

The Bowtun Loominary,

TUMFOWT TELEGRAPH,

UN LANKISHIRE LOOKIN-GLASS

[No. 1. JANUARY 5. 1861. [Vol. 13.

TH' HEDDITUR TO HIS READERS UN FRIENDS.

Allow me, good foak, before aw do owt else, to wish yoa, each un aw, a "Happy New Yer," un to deliver mysel uv a hope that before Owd Kesmus comes ogen yoa may meet wi plenty o good health un prosperity, un may feel yoarsels aw th' better, booath fizzically un morally, for th' herty good lowfs ut me un thoose ut may be good enough to become my assistants may provoke. Aw that th' strength of booath mind un buddy in maturity depends uppo this fust necessary operashun. Awd lickert ha forgetten one very desoirable thing, un that is a good understondin between mon un woife. Its uv mooar importance for married coupies to comprehend one another, than it is to be comprehended by any eawtsoiders wotever. Yoad better be a puzzle to oather a doctor, a peawson, a politishun, a lawyer, un a moral fillosofer.

The heading of Staton's *Bowtun Loominary*

On arrival he enquires of the organisers where he could find other members of his trade *"as I met as weel join 'em"*. He meets a steward for the demonstration who thought *"hond-loom weyvin had bin snuft eawt sometime sin – I assured him he wur mistaken for he'd a specimen o'th'craft befoor him."*[82]

[82] *Th'Lond-Tillers Lock-Eawt: Bobby Shuttle Wi'Th'Demonstrationists*, Bolton 1874

The caddy quilt weavers

Bobby was correct. Bolton still had a number of handloom-weavers, mostly working on quilts - the more 'fancy' end of the market. The fictitious Bobby Shuttle would have been one of them. Bolton developed a strong tradition specialising in caddow (or 'caddy') quilts. They may have been introduced to Bolton by refugees fleeing from persecution in Europe in the 18th century, or earlier. The mid-19th century marked the peak of caddow weaving in Bolton, and a powerful 'Counterpane Weavers' Association' existed for a time. [83]

Clarke said that "*Tonge Fold, historians show, was a noted handloom weaving village. Here, the now unpurchasable caddow counterpanes were made, and the Tonge Fold weavers were, it is said, the most truculent, quarrelsome crowd in the district.*"[84]

Clarke's friend John Kirkman's father (also called John) was a member of the association and wove the first Alhambra quilt, as well as the first fast-back quilt, to be made in Bolton, at Barlow and Jones' factory. He also kept a handloom in his cottage, reflecting the complex and prolonged transition from handloom to powerloom weaving in Bolton. [85]

Clarke mentions a handloom weavers' union banner in the possession of his friend: "*It shows the crude quilt-weaving on a Marseilles loom in use before the invention of the French 'Jacquard'. On top of the loom is the Bolton Borough Coat of Arms, an 'Elephant and Castle' (curious that Bolton is thus symbolically linked to India), and to the left a ship in full sail...*"[86]

A similar quilt, or possibly the same one, was presented by the union to Bolton's first coroner, Peter Taylor, is in the Bolton Museum's archives collection. It should be said that the counterpanes were anything but 'crude' and required great skill, which was unique to the Bolton weavers.

He describes the ancient tradition of 'Oak Apple Day' in the village, marking the anniversary of Charles II's escape from the Cromwellian armies at the Battle of

---

[83] The history of quilt ('counterpane') weaving in Bolton is fascinating. See Erin Beeston and Laurel Horton 'Bolton's Cotton Counterpanes: Hand-Weaving in the Industrial Age' in *Quilt Studies* 14, 2013. Thanks to Erin Beeston for background information

[84] Allen Clarke in *The Bolton Evening News*, May 29th 1928. Reprinted in *Lancashire Annual* 1928. He mentions the research of a Mr J. Bradburn who interviewed elderly villagers about the Oak Apple Day. Anna Bradburn was the last licensee of the Park View Inn so they could have been related

[85] Allen Clarke 'the Story of a Working Man – John Kirkman of Bolton' *Lancashire Annual* 1922

[86] *Moorlands* p.282

Worcester by hiding inside an oak tree. The weavers, and the village as a whole, celebrated the event in style. It was less a celebration of royalty than an excuse for a party. Weaving stopped for a week before the actual festival and large crowds came from around the area to sample the villagers' 'home brew'. The annual 'Nominy', a sort of rhymed proclamation, was read at each year's event and included the lines:

"The lively genius of Tonge Fold in trade,
Which has for many ages been,
As all the world throughout proclaim,
The first origin of counterpanes."

Bolton led the world in weaving counterpanes and it would seem that Tonge Fold was at the heart of it. In the early 19th century many Bolton counterpanes were exported to America and some are displayed in New England museums and New York's prestigious 'Met'. Many Bolton weavers emigrated to America and Canada in the early 19th century to pursue their craft.

More should be done to celebrate this heritage, but there are some examples of quilt-making to see. The new Bolton Interchange has an interesting contemporary art display on caddow quilts by artist Kate Maddison. They are near the main entrance on your left but easy to miss if you're running for your bus. Bolton Museum has a fine collection of caddows, dating back to 1794.

The place that made Clarke a household name

Clarke stated writing his *Tum Fowt Sketches* in the early 1890s, to lighten some of the rather heavy political articles in *The Labour Light*. According to Clarke, his printer suggested adding 'a bit o'dialect' to help popularise his message. Years later, he confessed that:

"I daresay Teddy Ashton's droll sketches have done more to help reforms than far more pretentious and direct articles. For 'Teddy', even in his comic sketches, pokes sly fun and undermining sarcasm at the iniquities and social injustices of the day."[87]

The 'penny readings' helped establish his reputation as a writer in the early 1890s. Clarke's main characters were Bill and Bet Spriggs, denizens of Tum Fowt and habitués of 'Th' Dug an' Kennel' pub, otherwise known as 'The Park View Inn'. The sketches were published separately as 'penny readings' and in newspapers and magazines, including his own *Northern Weekly* and *Lancashire Annuals*, but in many other publications as well, including *Liverpool Weekly Post*, *Cotton Factory Times* and *Yorkshire Factory Times*. They remain very funny and are best read out

[87] *Northern Weekly* August 26th 1905

loud in a gradely Lancashire accent. My favourites are ‘Bill Spriggs as a Minder’ and ‘Bill Spriggs as a Policeman’.

A contemporary postcard, c. 1895 of Allen Clarke (‘Teddy Ashton’) at The Dug an’ Kennel

Tonge Fold is also notable for being the location of Bolton’s first baby clinic, thanks to the work of the socialist, feminist and co-operator Sarah Reddish whom we’ll meet later. The clinic was established in 1908. Its work is perpetuated in the Tonge Fold Health Centre on Thicketford Road.

Tum Fowt in Modern Times

Today, ‘Tum Fowt’ is much-changed but the original ‘Dug an’ Kennel’ remains – the home of Bolton Labour councillor Elaine Sherrington, who is very aware of the history of the building and its place in Lancashire literature. An interesting connection to Allen Clarke is Elaine’s strongly-held spiritualist beliefs. Clarke’s book, *The Eternal Question*, is his well-argued testimony to support his belief in life after death. Staton lies buried nearby, in Tonge Cemetery.

13. Romantic Rivington and Horwich

'Gee up, my jolly owd hoss,
We're off to Rivington Pike,
Wi' brandysnaps and bottles o'pop,
Gee up, my jolly owd hoss'[88]

The reservoirs around Rivington and Anglezarke form Bolton's Lake District (though I'm sure Chorley will claim them as well). It was very much a popular local tourist destination back in Clarke's time, easily accessible by train or tram car to Horwich, with a walk from there to the barns and the pretty village of Rivington. Oddly, Clarke makes little mention of Rivington in *Moorlands and Memories*, apart from a rambling account of Lady Eleanor Willoughby who was around in the 17th century. Perhaps he thought Rivington, even then, was so popular it didn't need him to do anything more to sing its praises. He was also a friend of Lord Leverhulme who then owned the Rivington estate. Who was he?

Lord Leverhulme

William Hesketh Lever was born at 16 Wood Street, Bolton in 1851. By a strange irony, the birthplace of the capitalist *par excellence* has been home to Bolton Socialist Club since 1905. Lever was knighted in 1917 and chose the title 'Lord Leverhulme'. He bought the Rivington estate in 1900 and spent a fortune creating a park where there was once only rough moorland. It was his fantasy made real, with Japanese and Italian Gardens, ornamental lakes, a network of paths and the amazing seven-arched bridge. It was inspired by a Nigerian structure to which he dragged his newly-appointed stonemason Edward Hart 3000 miles to look at. And oh yes, there's that rather spooky-looking tower to which, I'm told, Lady Leverhulme used to enjoy retreating. She did her sewing in the upstairs room which was equipped with a fireplace. All very Gothic; but she had a fabulous view.

As large landowners go, Lever was perhaps one of the more enlightened. He was a Liberal and supported women's right to vote, though that didn't stop suffragette Edith Rigby from burning his house down in 1913. As acts of political violence go, it was on the 'softer' end of the spectrum. Before setting the house on fire she made sure there was nobody in, and up it went. But I wonder if, in her later years, she regretted her action? Burning people's houses down, whether you happen to be at home or not, is an act of violence; however justified the cause might be, the ends don't justify the means. But Rigby's actions were far less cruel than the treatment meted out to suffragettes on hunger strike, which was torture.

---

[88] Traditional, quoted in *Moorlands* p.341. See below

The Tower undergoing restoration

Lever was in some ways a good but dictatorial employer at his Port Sunlight factory, though there was another side to how he accrued his enormous wealth. He had extensive interests in the Belgian Congo, from 1911. He was complicit in the practice of 'forced labour', which was widely condemned. It can't be argued that this was 'normal' back then. Even by the standards of his day it was immoral and many Belgian figures protested against conditions on Lever's estates, to no effect. On the positive side, he did build houses and schools for the workforce; he was a classic benevolent despot. [89]

His attempt to transform the Hebridean island of Lewis - and in the process destroy the old crafting traditions - was not to his credit either but at least it could be argued it was in part motivated by a desire to improve life for the islanders, whether they wanted it or not!

Clarke had a good relationship with his lordship. He mentions Lever calling round to see his mother in Settle Street, Bolton, when he was visiting Lancashire on his return from Australia in 1924. He had met Clarke's younger brother Tom who was then editing *The Melbourne Herald*. As a 'thank you' to Lever, Clarke composed a dialect poem for him, entitled 'To a Gradely Gentlemon'![90]

Going up The Pike

Rivington Pike has long been regarded as a Bolton treasure. Each Good Friday – until 2020 at any rate – thousands of Boltonians would walk up George's Lane and on to the summit, taking advantage of burger bars and hot dog stands at the foot

---

[89] See J. Marchal *Leverhulme's Ghosts: colonial exploitation in the Congo,* 2008

[90] *Lancashire Annual,* 1924

of the Pike. It was always a 'popular' occasion, with some looking down on its supposed vulgarity. The Rivington 'Easter Fair' has a history stretching back to the early 19th century and probably earlier; a picture of the event was used as the frontispiece for *Moorlands and Memories*, taken by Clarke's friend R. Penketh, probably before the First World War.

The lines from the old children's song quoted above were still being sung in the 1960s. I wonder if they are now? If not, it would be a good project for local schools to revive the charming ditty. Clarke was very familiar with the Pike and mentions a lonely house – the former 'Sportsman's Arms', then (according to Clarke) home to a recluse who may have suffered from leprosy. The pub must have offered a welcome stop for walkers and wanderers. It closed in 1876 and became known as Sportsman's Cottage. The original building was demolished around the time of the First World War and the building that stands today - 'Pike Cottage' – was built in 1920.

There is a delightful outdoor cafe – The Pike Snack Shack - next door, with tables and benches to sit out and admire the view over Horwich and across to Southport and the sea. It's popular with walkers and cyclists making their way up to The Pike or Two Lads. The 'snack shack' is run by Andy and Leonie who bought Pike Cottage in March 2020 and wasted no time getting the business up and running. As a 'takeaway' facility it was able to keep going during the Lockdown. My mate Nigel was delighted to discover they do those well-known Bolton delicacies, Carr's pasties.

Rivington Pike isn't widely known for its industrial heritage, but back in Allen Clarke's day the area around the Pike and Winter Hill was a hive of industry – coal mines, brick works and quarries. The remains of the former tramway that ran down from Wildersmoor Colliery are still visible in part. The coal mine and other surrounding pits have been well documented by Horwich Heritage. The last colliery, Montcliffe, closed in 1966.[91]

The Gardens - and Bolton as it might have been

Leverhulme, or Lever, was a complex person. His outstanding achievements were the creation of the 'model village' at Port Sunlight and the gardens at Rivington. It's possible that Hall i'th'Wood may not have survived demolition without the restoration work he carried out. He gifted 'Lever Park' – the lower part of the

---

[91] See Dave Lane, Derek Cartwright and Garry Rhodes *Winter Hill and Anglezarke Scrapbook*, Bolton 2019, for information about the mines and quarries around Winter Hill. Horwich Heritage has lots more archive material and the Heritage Centre is now open three days a week – check their website for details

estate bordering on the reservoir – to the people of Bolton.

The gardens were designed by the brilliant landscape architect T.H. Mawson, who also produced visionary ideas for Bolton town centre in a series of lectures entitled *Bolton as it is and as it might be* (see Chapter 23). Allen Clarke was an enthusiastic supporter, commenting *"if only the marvellous Mr Mawson can manage to get Bolton shaped according to his great town-planning dream I for one will join in due song of thanksgiving."*[92]

Once again, Lever was involved with the plans which would have transformed Bolton into a magnificent city with fine tree-lined boulevards. And we wouldn't have ended up with 1960s aberrations. But hey ho, it wasn't to be. But what we did get were the gardens.[93]

After Lever's death his family decided to sell the estate to brewer John Magee. After his death it passed to Liverpool Corporation who presided over its steady decline into ruin. The revival began in recent years thanks to the efforts of Rivington Heritage Trust and a large team of volunteers, working closely with the current landowners United Utilities and helped by a generous grant from the Heritage Lottery Fund. It is coming back into its own, for everyone to enjoy. Who knows, maybe we'll even see the return of pagodas in the future?

The many sides of Horwich

There are several sides to Horwich, at least three with the further addition of the huge 'retail park' at Middlebrook. The original settlement was a small village that grew up around the bleaching industry at Wallsuches, owned by the Ridgway family. Horwich had a thriving handloom-weaving industry in the late 18th century and the attractive stone terraces around George Street and Chapel Street are classic weavers' cottages, known as 'The Club Houses'. There was small-scale coal-mining and extensive quarrying on the slopes of Rivington Pike. Quarrying is still very much an active industry in the area, with a large but well-hidden quarry off George's Lane.

The Loco Works

The 'second Horwich', ironically, has largely disappeared. This was the Horwich of the late 19th and 20th centuries, based on the huge locomotive works which opened in the mid-1880s. It produced all of the Lancashire and Yorkshire Railway's large fleet of locomotives, as well as carriages. The L&Y (or 'owd Lanky')

---

92 *Moorlands* p.147

93 See *Bolton News* August 15th 2020 'Looking Back' supplement

amalgamated with its rival London and North Western Railway in 1922, quickly followed by absorption into the London Midland and Scottish Railway.

An aerial view of the Loco Works in its heyday. *Courtesy Horwich Heritage*

The 'Works' continued to build and repair locos and carriages through to the 1960s. During the First and Second World War production turned over to tanks, guns and shells. The railway factory wasn't the only heavy industry in the town. De Havilland built their factory close to the loco works and probably poached some of the skilled workers. There was some cotton manufacturing, little trace of which remains. But above all, Horwich became world-famous as a 'railway town'.[94]

A Lancashire and Yorkshire Railway freight loco under repair at Horwich Loco Works. *Courtesy Horwich Heritage*

[94] My novel *The Works* (Lancashire Loominary, 2020) is partly about the Locomotive Works and life in the factory in the 1970s and 1980s

Clarke was ambivalent about railways and steam locomotives. He made clear his hatred of the industrialism and pollution which the 'Steam Age' inflicted on Lancashire. But he couldn't hide his fascination with railways. In one of his early novels, *The Knobstick*, set during the 1887 Engineer's Strike in Bolton, the hero, Harry Belton, is out for a walk and pauses on 'a little rustic bridge in the heart of a sweet valley' – probably 'Bonny Lasses Bridge', just north of Lostock Junction. A train shoots by and Belton reflects, in Whitmanite mode:

"Great and wonderful is man who conceived and constructed the railway train! It is almost alive! It flies along of itself, and carries its maker in its arms like a child! How beautiful! How glorious is the locomotive! The lightning on wheels! The horse made divine! Mighty and sublime must be he who made the locomotive! Then how much more mighty and sublime must that Power be which made him who made the locomotive! There must be a God!" [95]

The men who designed and built those locomotives lived and worked within a few hundred yards of where Harry was reflecting on the meaning of life and a God whose existence was confirmed by the steam locomotive.

The Loco Works closed in 1983, though many of the houses where those men and their families lived, still stand. The small terraced streets are named after the great engineers – Watt, Siemens, Arkwright, Brunel and many more. The magnificent Victorian villas which were home to some of the great names in railway engineering – Aspinall, Hughes and others – can be seen along Chorley New Road, alongside mansions owned by the big cotton barons. No wonder Clarke dubbed it 'the road of riches and romance'.

Horwich Loco Works in its final months. The Erecting Shop (or 'Carriage Shop') in 1983

[95] *The Knobstick: a story of love and labour*, Manchester 1891 p.108

Horwich is proud of its railway history and the Heritage Centre has a fine display of models, photographs and documents from the town's years of glory as one of the world's great locomotive centres. I 'served my time' there briefly, in the mid-70s. I was mostly employed in the Spring Smithy, which was hard, dirty and dangerous. But the men I worked with were fantastic. Some of that experience formed the basis of my novel *The Works*.

What Clarke would have made of 'Middlebrook' isn't hard to imagine. He would have hated its consumerism. He would have lamented the dominance of the car. He would have been appalled by the cheap-jack 'architecture', if you can call it that, with perhaps the exception of the football stadium. So let's get away from here and find some fresh air. You don't have to go far.

Headless Cross and its travels

Less than two miles from Middlebrook is Rivington Reservoir, a popular spot for over a century. There are some fascinating by-ways and places of interest en route that are off the beaten track. Not least 'Headless Cross' in Grimeford. It's just off the main Chorley Road, near the old Millstone pub, now an Italian restaurant. According to George Birtill, the original 'head' of Headless Cross was St Anthony, reflecting the area's strong Catholic tradition. The head was probably removed at the time of Henry VIII and the pillar was used a signpost. It seems that the pillar was removed during the construction of nearby Rivington Reservoir and ended up at Ridgmont Park. It then progressed to a higher level, to Rivington Bungalow in Lord Leverhulme's grounds.

However, George Birtill tells us that: *"It was not until 1945, chiefly due to the agitation of Mr C.F. Sixsmith, who represented Anderton on the Rural District Council, that it was restored to its present position."*[96]

Good old Charlie! This was of course Charles Sixsmith, Whitmanite and textile magnate, close friend of Edward Carpenter as well as long-term chairman of Chorley Rural District Council, whom we shall meet in the next chapter. He lived just along the lane from Headless Cross at 'Brownlow', a house designed by the eminent architect and fellow Whitman admirer Charles Holden, in 1907.

A 2020 view of Headless Cross

[96] George Birtill *The Enchanted Hills*, Preston 1966, p.80

Lancashire's herbalist tradition

Instead of heading north towards Anderton and Rivington, take the lane southwards, crossing the main Chorley to Bolton road. You will go past a small group of houses – Grimeford village - which is home to 'medical herbalist' Andrea Downey. She represents an old Lancashire tradition and one that Clarke did much to promote.

His *Northern Weekly* and *Lancashire Annuals* often featured adverts for herbalists, including the redoubtable Hassall of Farnworth, who had a shop and practice on Longcauseway. Bolton was home to the doyen of medical herbalists Richard Lawrence Hool, the author of several widely-respected books. [97]The family stall in Bolton Market still continues, on a limited basis. It was first established in 1868.

LANCASHIRE ANNUAL. 61

Over 30 years ago Dr. Hassall advertised in Teddy's publications.

YOU KNOW HASSALL !

HASSALL'S Supply the World with
HERBAL MEDICINES
—Cheaply, Palatably, Efficiently.—

Take **HASSALL'S D.W. HERBS.** Post Free **7½d.** **D.W.** 6 Packets Post Free **3/4** 12 Packets Post Free **6/6**

For
DROPSY, LIVER, KIDNEYS, & BLADDER.

D.W. THE BAG THAT'S BRAVED THE
——BATTLE AND THE BREEZE——
TAKE D.W. AND LAUGH AT THE PANEL!

Hassall's business was Established in 1864. The present proprietor (Son of THE Dr. Hassall) was born in the Herbal Profession over 36 years ago! He did not jump into it from another job!! Herbalism is his life-long occupation.

Three useful Books on Herbs, post free, **3d.**: or Four Books (all different) for **4d.** Information in them worth their weight in gold.

Over **300 SPECIFIC PREPARATIONS** on hand. Send for list.

HASSALL IS THE MAN TO CURE YOUR COMPLAINTS.

Send Stamp for particulars and state your case to:

DR. HASSALL, Dispensary, Farnworth, Nr. Bolton.

An advert for Hassall's shop, from *Teddy Ashton's Lancashire Annual*

Last of the great Lancashire Herbalists: Hool's shop in Bolton Market, 2019

[97] R.L. Hool *British Wild Herbs and Common Plants, Their Uses in Medicine,* Southport 1924

The Bolton Lake District

The reservoirs of Rivington and Anglezarke add up to what can justly be called 'Bolton's Lake District'. Although they are not natural lakes, their location, with Rivington Pike rising up behind, make them very beautiful. It's possible to walk around all of them and United Utilities has done a good job in making them accessible.

The area has become enormously popular, though even in Clarke's day it was well-visited. There are several places where you can enjoy a snack or a full meal – the Rivington barns, Spring Cottage, the Rivington Tea Rooms in the Unitarian Chapel grounds and the Bowling Club. Further up towards the Pike is the 'Snack Shack' which has the best view of the lot.

Rivington Chapel is one of those very special places with so many historical connections it deserves a book of its own. Charles Sixsmith and his wife Lucy are buried here, with fellow Whitmanite Rev. Samuel Thompson. Look out for the plaque at the entrance to the chapel grounds celebrating its 'Whitman' heritage. The adjoining tea room is a classic traditional walkers' and cyclists' haven (or heaven!) offering substantial and tasty food.

The 'Face in The Wall'

There are two, or maybe three main reservoirs if you count Rivington as being a couple, Lower and Upper, separated by Horrobin Lane causeway. North of the Rivington Reservoirs is Anglezarke. There are two smaller 'lakes' – Yarrow and High Bullough, each with their own charm. Although the roads around Rivington can be extremely busy, you don't have to go far to 'get away from it all'.

Angelzarke is an area of great beauty, perhaps at its best in Autumn

Yarrow is interesting for its 'face in the wall' – the very corroded impression of a human face carved by one of the stonemason's when the reservoir was being built in the mid-1860s. Legend has it that the effigy is based on an unpopular foreman who made the lives of the workers hell! It has been damaged and at one point was removed to Great House Barn tourist information office for its protection. Quite rightly, it's back in its proper place, you don't want a 'Timberbottom Skulls' situation developing, do you? See Chapter 15 if you're wondering what I'm on about. It's near to the overflow down to Anglezarke Reservoir and takes some searching. To give you a clue, it's on the side looking up towards Rivington Pike.

14. Afoot with the Whitmanites

"it is fitting that Bolton should be distinguished above all towns in England by having a group of Whitman enthusiasts, for many years in close touch, by letter and visit, with 'the Master'. For I am sure Walt Whitman, the singer of out-door life, would have loved to ramble on our Lancashire moorlands."[98]

Bolton, and Rivington in particular, are closely connected with that great American poet of the 19th century, Walt Whitman. *Leaves of Grass* has been translated into most world languages (but not Lancashire dialect) and literary scholars in his home nation applaud him as the singer of a democratic America. His close connections with Bolton are a fascinating aspect of the life of 'the good grey poet'.

'Wallace' and friends

Why here? Towards the end of his life, Whitman (1819-1892) developed a close friendship with a small group of admirers in Bolton who jokingly called themselves 'The Eagle Street College' after the modest two-up two-down terraced house in The Haulgh where the group's mentor, J.W. Wallace, lived with his parents in the mid-1880s. They met each week to discuss literature, philosophy and whatever took their fancy. The Whitman connection started with a birthday greeting sent to him in 1885 signed by Wallace and his friend and 'deputy' in the group Dr John Johnston, a respected local GP whom we'll meet again later. The terrace is long gone but there's a plaque on the brick building where the house stood.

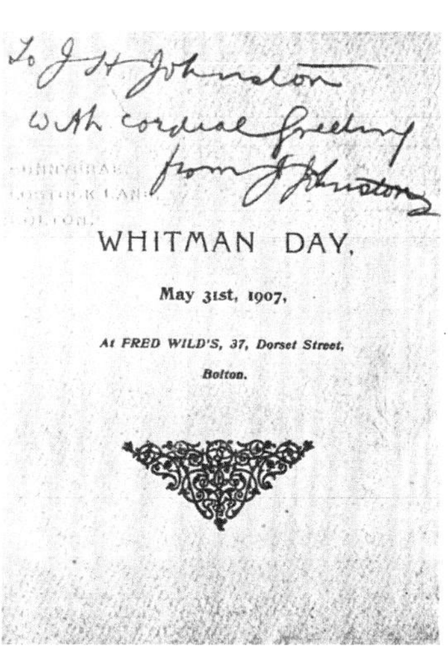
WHITMAN DAY,
May 31st, 1907,
At FRED WILD'S, 37, Dorset Street,
Bolton.

Invitation card to a Whitman Day picnic at Fred Wild's, 1907

The term 'guru' could accurately be applied to Wallace. He was a deeply spiritual person and eagerly adopted Whitman's blend of eastern philosophy and love of nature. One member of the group, Wentworth Dixon described him as *"the very embodiment of the perfect friend"* adding *"I only wish I had the ability to portray to you the almost unique man he was – the nobility and beauty of his personality, his loving kindness, sympathy and helpfulness to everyone regardless of condition."* [99]

---

98 *Moorlands* p.63

99 Paul Salveson *With Walt Whitman in Bolton: spirituality, sex and socialism in a Northern mill town* Bolton 2019 (4th ed.)

He worked for most of his life as an architect's assistant with the famous Bolton firm of Bradshaw, Gass and Hope. He moved to a small terraced house in Anderton in the early 1890s to get away from Bolton's smoke and grime and so he could be on the edge of the moorland he loved so much.

Clarke was a good friend of Wallace's, both being active members of Bolton Labour Church and sharing a similar 'spiritual' idea of socialist politics. He often called in to see Wallace when cycling to or from Blackpool. [100]

Distinguished visitors to Babylon Lane

His modest home at 40 Babylon Lane became an international centre of radical politics and culture, with visits from Keir Hardie, founder of the Labour Party, John and Katherine Bruce Glasier and many other leading figures in the early socialist movement. Visitors from the USA and Canada were not uncommon. Dr Richard Maurice Bucke, a close friend of Whitman's, came in 1894. In 1913 the American free thinker, poet and anarchist J.W. Lloyd visited Rivington and met the Whitman group, including Allen Clarke. A plaque above the door celebrates Wallace and his Whitman connections.

Clarke recalls in *Moorlands and Memories*: *"...a ramble in 1913 with the Bolton 'Whitmanites' and friends, including poet Lloyd from New Jersey, up Babylon Lane and across the fields to Rivington, to celebrate the birthday of the great American singer of comradeship and immortality. It was May 31st, but we had rain and hail and thunder that day – and then sunshine. But we enjoyed 'the gleesome saunter o'er fields and hillsides', and after a tour of Lever Park, where the Waste Merchant commented in his own droll way on the outdoor menageries – we had tea at the foot of the Pike in the Old Manse of the Rev. S. Thompson, our genial Scotch host."* [101]

Readings from *Leaves of Grass* were followed by a speech from Wallace. A 'loving cup', a gift from Whitman's American friends, was passed around the assemblage, containing spiced claret. Members of the party sported lilacs in their jackets, Whitman's favourite flower immortalised in his elegy on the death of Lincoln, 'When Lilacs Last in the Dooryard Bloomed'.

In the early days, it was very much an all-male thing, with the one woman in the group being Minnie Whiteside, Wallace's housekeeper who looked after him at his home in Anderton. After his death she became the lynchpin of the Bolton Whitmanite group, but managed to fall out with Charlie Sixsmith.

---

[100] *Moorlands* p.62

[101] *Moorlands* pp.62-3

Fred Wild – cycling companion

The 'waste merchant' alluded to in Clarke's description of the day was Fred Wild. He was a jovial, down-to-earth character who ran a cotton waste business on Phoenix Street, off Folds Road. He was a keen cyclist and member of the Labour Church and Independent Labour Party. Clarke's description is affectionate: *"He is one of the merriest cusses you ever met...There is also some poetic spirit in him – we are all fearful and wonderful mixtures – which expresses itself in the use of the artist's brush. He is a disciple of Walt Whitman, and has democratic ideals."*[102]

In Clarke's second volume of *Windmill Land* he describes a bike ride with Fred from Knott End to Pilling on a wet and wild October day. The pair cycle to Fleetwood and get the ferry to Knott End, experiencing a decidedly rough crossing. They get as far as Pilling with numerous adventures and conversations on the way, including Whitman's view of the relationship between town and country, which Wild describes as 'like whisky and soda'. By early evening they had had enough cycling and took the Garstang and Knott End Railway back to the ferry, with another lively crossing - *"the waves splashed over the little steamer as it plodded across."*[103]

Charles Sixsmith: textile magnate and libertarian socialist

Another fascinating member of the group, born and bred in Anderton, was Charles Sixmith. He rose to a senior position in the Lancashire cotton industry, managing Bentinck Mill in Farnworth, which specialised in the West African trade. He became very close to Edward Carpenter following their meeting at a Whitman gathering in Rivington in 1891. He frequently went on holiday with Carpenter and his lover George Merrill and it is likely that they were more than 'just friends'. He was another complex person.

He married Lucy in 1908. Sixsmith served on Chorley Rural District Council for 37 years, rising to become chairman in the 1940s. He died at the age of 83 in 1954 and is buried, with his wife, in the graveyard at Rivington Unitarian Chapel.

He became a distinguished figure in local government. In 1915 he played an active part in the defence of local footpaths when Liverpool Corporation attempted to close some of the reservoir paths around Rivington. He was an authority on textile design and had progressive views on industrial relations in the textile industry. He built up a large collection of Whitman artefacts and letters which are now

---

[102] *More Windmill Land* ,1918, p.371, in chapter entitled 'A Wild Day with the Waste Merchant'

[103] *More Windmill Land* p.378

available in Manchester's John Rylands Library.

He was an environmentalist before his time, serving on the executive of the North-West branch of the Council for the Preservation of Rural England for many years. He campaigned against pollution and the incursion of motor traffic. It's sadly ironic that the M61 was constructed alongside his fine house, Brownlow. What a fight he would have put up to stop it, had he still been alive in the late 1960s.

The quintessential Whitman garden party: on The Rev. Thompson's lawn, Rivington, in 1894.A young Sixsmith on the far right. Edward Carpenter immediately behind

There are many echoes of Rivington's Whitman connections at the wonderful Unitarian chapel by the village green. As well as Thompson and Sixsmith being buried there, there is one of the series of 'Walt Whitman' plaques by the chapel gate, thanks to the work of Jacqueline Dagnall. The Rev. Thompson's rectory, pictured at the 1894 garden party is privately occupied but visible from the Belmont road (Sheep House Lane), just above the tea rooms.

A Harwood Poet, Suffragist and Whitmanite

In later years, women played an increasingly prominent role in the Whitman 'Fellowship'. Wallace's housekeeper, Minnie Whiteside, kept the Whitman flame burning in Bolton long after Wallace's death. Another highly talented member of the group was Alice Collinge, who lived at Riding Gate, Harwood, for most of her life and was an active member of the Lancashire Authors Association which Clarke had established in 1909.

She was a teacher and active in the women's suffrage movement and the Independent Labour Party. She was the resident organist at Bolton Labour Church in the early 1900s when Clarke was involved, and met 'the rebel countess' Constance Markievicz, the first woman elected as an MP to the UK parliament. As a Sinn Fein member she did not take her seat. Alice also met Edward Carpenter, Eva Gore-Booth and Adela Pankhurst through her political activities. In her autobiographical notes, she tells this charming story of the Bolton Whitman group and Wallace in particular:

"As a counter-attraction to those hectic days, there was the restful contemplative influence of the Whitman Fellowship behind it all, and in that influence alone, I owe an eternal debt to Bolton. To hear the late J.W. Wallace read a paper on Whitman, in a Whitman atmosphere, either at Rivington, Walker Fold or The Haulgh, was a perfect inspiration, and one of those special privileges that one cannot account for."[104]

Probably the last photograph of the original cast...at John Ormrod's house, Walker Fold, c. 1924. Wallace and Johnston were both elderly and in poor health. By this time, the group had many more women members, including Alice Collinge, seated on the far right. Ormrod (the tallest member of the group) at the back of the group

---

[104] *Autobiographical Notes* – manuscript in Bolton Library and Archives

Alice won several poetry prizes and lectured for the Workers' Educational Association on English Literature. She was an active member of the Lancashire Authors' Association, being elected deputy chairman (sic). In her later years was appointed a governor of Bolton School. She made a great contribution to Bolton's political, social and cultural life, dying in 1957.

The Whitman tradition continues

The group built up a strong relationship with many of Whitman's American friends which continued decades after the poet's death. It is perpetuated in the strong links today between Bolton and American Whitman scholars who are regular visitors to the town. Bolton Public Library is immensely proud of its priceless Whitman Collection which is more well-used than it has ever been, assisted by growing interest from the University of Bolton in the town's Whitman connection.

Passing round 'the Loving Cup' – an early revived Whitman Day, late 1980s

The 'Whitman Day' celebrations were revived in the mid-1980s by members of Bolton Socialist Club, supported by Bolton Library. The first walk took place in 1984; the following year American Whitman scholar Ed Folsom took part in the walk. In the first few years of the revival the historic three-handled loving cup from 1894 was given parole from its home in Bolton Museum and allowed out, fulfilling its traditional role of getting the members slightly tiddly on spiced claret or a suitable substitute. Concerns about the safety of the cup led to it being confined to its museum home, with less prosaic cups being used. More recently a replacement 'loving cup' was procured, not dissimilar to the original.

In the first decade or so the event ebbed and flowed, with a few years being missed. It has now established itself as a regular event, maintained by members of Bolton Socialist Club, particularly its chair Chris Chilton and Stuart Murray.[105]

In the 21st century, Lancashire's Whitmanites are often joined by American guests, still celebrating the poet's birthday with a walk on the Rivington moors, often hosted by the Unitarian chapel. True to tradition, they wear sprigs of lilac and take turns to read their favourite Whitman poems. It's a unique aspect of the North's cultural heritage and very much alive.

The year 2019 was the bi-centenary of Whitman's birth and Bolton hosted a three-day Whitman festival over his 'birthday weekend' with a major international conference hosted by the University of Bolton and events at the Socialist Club.

On May 31st, 2020, Whitmanites from Bolton and the United States joined up through a 'zoom' conference to read Whitman poems and celebrate his enduring legacy.

The new generation of 'Whitmanites' assembled at Barrow Bridge before setting off on the annual walk

---

[105] Chris has recently ventured into poetry. His collection *How to count trees and other poems* was published in 2020

15. Civil War and Civic Pride: from Churchgate to Bromley Cross and Turton Tower

"There is much history about this Turton Tower, with its quaint black and white, wood and plaster, gabled architecture, and the old sun-dial on the lawn, and also – so tradition runs, a ghost, a rustling lady in white."[106]

For the cyclist, the journey from Bolton to Turton Tower is demanding. It's a long drag up Tonge Moor Road, followed by more climbing after what used to be 'The Royal Oak' in Clarke's day, but is now 'Roka', at the junction of Turton Road and Rigby Road, Bradshaw. It was also the tram terminus. Clarke loved a good yarn and this particular journey has quite a few - ancient and more recent, tragic as well as amusing.

The Bolton Massacre

Starting at the town centre, the junction of Churchgate, Deansgate, Bradshawgate and Bank Street is a place of great historical interest. The 'Market Cross' by the junction chronicles Bolton's history with descriptive plaques on each of its four sides. Close by is the town's oldest pub, The Man and Scythe, which dates back to the 13th century; it was mentioned in records from 1251. It is well known as the place where, in October 1651, the 7th Earl of Derby had his last drink before being executed for his part in the infamous 'Massacre of Bolton' seven years earlier.

The story of Bolton and the English Civil War is well documented; it fascinated Clarke. His first novel, published in 1891, was *The Lass at the Man and Scythe* and is set at the time of the civil war. He reworked it as *John o'God's Sending* which he published in 1924. In more recent years, Les Smith made the story into a play which was performed at Bolton's Octagon Theatre.

The massacre that took place in Bolton in 1644 was shocking, even by today's standards of war crimes and genocide. The town – well-known for its republican sentiments and called 'The Geneva of the North' - was besieged by Royalist troops under the command of the Earl. After a strong defence the town was over-run and a massacre ensued; women and children were not spared. The Earl was tried and found guilty, being sentenced to death and executed in Bolton on October 15th 1651 by James Whowell, a Bolton farmer who lived above Edgworth. The axe which beheaded the Earl stayed in the family for many years before being sold.

---

[106] *Moorlands* p.211

Clarke is generous in his assessment of the Earl. He writes "*...to judge by what I have read of him, he seems to have been a cultured and kindly sort of man...The big fault with him was that he was on the wrong side in the Civil War. He was on the side of royal tyranny and aristocratic arrogance opposed to the government and the people.*" [107]

Bolton 'Trottin'

By the junction of Churchgate, Bradshawgate and Deansgate is The Swan Hotel, another well-known Bolton institution. Clarke describes the origin of 'Bowton Trottin' which, so the story goes, was the result of an entertaining incident in the hotel. In the early 18th century a rather arrogant visitor from 'down south' (sometimes said to be only as far 'south' as Manchester) was staying in the hotel and clearly got on the nerves of some of the locals with tales of his great feats and achievements. One of the locals bet him he could hold his foot on a tub of boiling water longer than any man in the world. The visitor took him up on his challenge and two tubs of boiling water were brought from the kitchen. The visitor quickly withdrew his foot from the tub, while the local sat there smiling, with his leg in the hot water, 'placidly puffing his pipe'. Clarke describes the outcome – with the traveller being amazed at his rival's endurance. It turned out that the Bolton chap had a wooden leg, revealed to laughter from the locals and annoyance to the deflated visitor. As Clarke drolly comments, 'thus was the traveller trotted'.

Clarke made much of the theme and published a satirical local newspaper in the early 1890s called *The Trotter*, which pre-figured *Teddy Ashton's Journal* and *Teddy Ashton's Northern Weekly*. However, he wasn't the first. As we've seen in Chapter 12 J.T. Staton published his *Bowtun Trotter un Tum Fowt Telegraph* back in the 1850s.

The Unitarian Tradition in Bolton

Bank Street is an old Bolton thoroughfare with much history to it; it's currently going through some major changes. On the left going down the hill is Bank Street Unitarian Chapel where the Bolton Whitmanites used to meet. The chapel continues the Unitarian tradition of tolerance, inclusivity and liberal Christianity. Long may it do so. There is a plaque outside the chapel celebrating its Whitman connections.

Further down on the right is the site of the former 'Top Storey Club' which had a calamitous fire on May 1st 1961, taking the lives of 19 men and women.

---

[107] *Moorlands* p.203

This whole area is part of a major redevelopment which will see the River Croal transformed from being an open sewer in years gone by into an important feature of the town's regeneration. It can't come soon enough.

Parson Folds and a draughty signalbox

Coming out of Bolton towards Tonge Moor, the busy road is named after Parson Folds, another Bolton 'character' whom Clarke loved to write about. He was a contemporary of Samuel Crompton and officiated at the inventor's wedding to Mary Pimlott. He preached at St Anne's church, Chapeltown, and used to ride up this road on horseback, stopping off to 'camp' with some of the locals on his way.

The road drops down under the viaduct which carries the Bolton to Blackburn railway, and the former branch line to Halliwell Sidings and Astley Bridge station, which opened in 1877 and closed two years later, unable to face tram competition.

The daily freight from Burnden Yard comes off the main line to Halliwell Sidings, c 1977

The goods yard carried on until 1981. I remember it well - I was signalman at Astley Bridge Junction, perched high on top of the viaduct where the two lines split. It could be a draughty place, but the views across Bolton and up to the moors, were splendid. Down below the viaduct was the famous Ryder's engineering works, long since gone. My first job after opening the signalbox each morning, at 07.20, was to brew up and boil an egg for my breakfast. After this modest repast I would flick the egg shells over the viaduct into the works yard below. This wasn't well received by Ryder's employees. I received my comeuppance by getting a good telling-off by Brian Northey, one of Ryder's shop stewards, at a meeting of Bolton Trades Council.

The Accursed Inventor

Samuel Crompton, the unfortunate inventor of the spinning mule, has close connections with this area. He was born in Firwood Fold, a delightful spot off Tonge Moor Road, near the junction with Crompton Way. Hall'i'th'Wood is on the opposite side of Tonge Moor Road, off Crompton Way - reached by a right turn after passing under the railway bridge. Crompton lived here for many years and was where he invented his 'mule' that transformed the fortunes of the Lancashire cotton industry. He got very little benefit from it.

Crompton was a tragic figure whose story fascinated Clarke. He wove the story of Crompton's invention and his life in poverty, into a novel *Black Slaves and White – or Samuel Crompton, Inventor*, serialised in *Northern Weekly* during but never published as a book[108]. The same tale may have been re-used as *The Accursed Inventor*, published in 1904[109]. The hall was bought by William Lever in 1899 who restored it as a museum and donated it to the people of Bolton in 1902; it remains in the ownership of Bolton Council. Both Firwood Fold and Hall i'th'Wood are well worth visiting. The hall is, at least in normal times, open to the public on certain days.

Timberbottom skulls and a pretty arboretum

Make a further stop at the junction of the Turton and Harwood roads, by the old tram terminus at what was The Royal Oak. Nearby is 'The Bolton Arboretum' which lies behind the old pub and stretches down to the River Tonge. The arboretum was developed in recent years by Bolton Council and is a lovely place to visit in Spring-time.

Just along the river towards Bolton is the old hamlet of 'Timberbottom' famous for its legend of 'the Timberbottom Skulls' which Clarke wrote about. In the mists of time two skulls were placed on the mantelpiece of the farm house, with the injunction, handed down over the years, never to remove them. Of course, someone did, thinking it more appropriate to have them buried in Bradshaw Chapel graveyard.

'Nowt but trouble' ensued and they were quickly replaced in their original position and Timberbottom returned to quiet normality. When the farm was demolished

---

[108] *Northern Weekly*, first instalment September 11th 1897

[109] *Northern Weekly* July 30th 1904

the skulls transferred to the more commodious surroundings of Bradshaw Hall where they seemed to be quite content, apart from an occasion when one had to be sent to Manchester for repair and all hell broke loose. The skulls are now kept at Turton Tower and calm has returned, for the time being. The skulls rest on the bible from Bradshaw Hall. In addition, the datestone from Timberbottom Farm was relocated in front of the tower, so the skulls should feel at home.

The Jumbles, change for the better?

There is a good alternative to using the busy Turton Road towards Bromley Cross. Drop down the road towards Harwood and turn left after crossing the bridge. There is a lovely path that takes you up to the Jumbles reservoir through a *"glen of rocks and waters..though spoiled now by the works which foul the stream along whose bank you may walk to Turton Bottoms, the other end of The Jumbles."*[110]

Clarke is referring to what was the extensive Bradshaw Bleachworks, responsible – in Clarke's time – for the pollution. The works closed in the 1970s and lay derelict for many years. Most of the site was cleared though some of the original fine stone buildings were kept and now form part of a residential development which was sensitively designed. In Clarke's time the delightful glen – or clough – continued through The Jumbles and on to Turton Bottoms. Today, part of the walk is alongside Jumbles Reservoir.

The upper end of the clough was dammed and flooded in the late 1960s; the reservoir was opened by the Queen in 1971. It was sad to lose the Jumbles clough though the reservoir offers an attractive walk with cafes at the adjacent 'Fisheries' and by the side of the reservoir.

Bromley Cross station and the nervous Nelsonians

If you stick to the road and turn right after the railway bridge, you'll pass Bromley Cross station, with its pedestrian level crossing. It features in one of Clarke's ('Teddy Ashton') *Tum Fowt Sketches* – 'Sammy Snokes' Donkey An Th' Express Train'. It's a tale about a stubborn mule which insists on sitting down across the tracks, as a fast train approaches. Fortunately, after much heaving and pushing, the mule escapes the oncoming train in the nick of time.

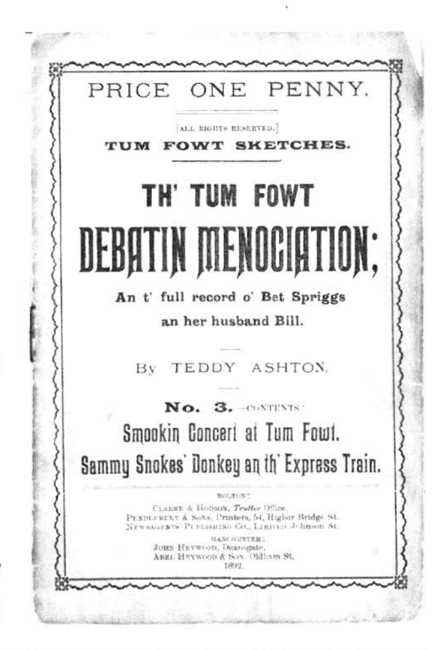
PRICE ONE PENNY.

[ALL RIGHTS RESERVED.]

TUM FOWT SKETCHES.

TH' TUM FOWT

DEBATIN MENOCIATION;

An t' full record o' Bet Spriggs
an her husband Bill.

By TEDDY ASHTON.

No. 3.—CONTENTS:

Smookin Concert at Tum Fowt.

Sammy Snokes' Donkey an th' Express Train.

BOLTON:
CLARKE & HODSON, *Trotter* Office.
PENDLEBURY & SONS, Printers, 54, Higher Bridge St.
NEWSAGENTS' PUBLISHING CO., LIMITED, Johnson St.
MANCHESTER:
JOHN HEYWOOD, Deansgate.
ABEL HEYWOOD & SON, Oldham St.
1892.

'Sammy Snokes' Donkey an' th' Express Train' by Teddy Ashton. Published in *Tum Fowt Sketches* No. 3, 1892

[110] *Moorlands* p. 209

The adjacent Railway Hotel re-opened in 2019 and has a strong 'railway' flavour. Many years ago I was a guard working a holiday special back from Southport to Nelson and we were stopped at Bromley Cross waiting for a train coming off the single line from Darwen. The signalman told us we'd be about 25 minutes. I advised the passengers of the situation and suggested they might like to have a quick 'gill' in The Railway across the road. Only two people responded to the invitation, who happened to be the driver and guard of the train (something you would never do today). The Nelsonians must have been worried about missing their train home and being stranded in this strange land. Though how it could have set off without its driver and guard didn't seem to have entered their calculations.

A diesel loco-hauled Blackburn to Manchester train arrives at Bromley Cross, c1987, over the infamous level crossing immortalised in the tale of Sammy Snokes' Donkey

If you're on your bike, the hard climbing starts again, up to Haydock Lane and past the pretty row of cottages on the left, then dropping down by 'The King Bill' – the King William IV pub – where the road burrows under the railway and then climbs sharply again up to the entrance to Turton Tower.

The station at Bromley Cross is a good place to start a walk along Jumbles Reservoir, if you cross the tracks at the level crossing (avoiding any approaching expresses) and stroll up Grange Road. You can loop round the reservoir using the footbridge at the head of the lake, or continue on to either Turton Tower passing the war-time pill-box or continue along 'the old Jumbles' towards Edgworth.

Turton Tower's attractions and importance

Turton Tower's history, Clarke tells us, goes back to 1101 "*originally occupied by a family named Orrell, who came over with that wholesale robber, known in history as William the Conqueror.*" Clarke is more kindly disposed towards a later owner in the early 17th century, Sir Humphrey Chetham, a fustian merchant who endowed Chetham's College in Manchester for boy orphans. He bought the Tower in 1628 but never lived there. The school opened in 1653 and still flourishes as an outstanding centre of musical excellence. J.T. Staton, of 'Bowtun Trotter' fame, was one of its products.

Clarke says of Chetham that he *"may be truly termed Lancashire's pioneer philanthropist, setting England one of earliest noble examples of how a rich man may use his wealth in a Christian way for the help and good of his fellow folk."* [111]

Turton Tower itself is a fine building, with various extensions added over the centuries. It is in a delightful setting of woodland bounded by the railway. The path beyond the hall takes you up towards the old station and on to either Chapeltown village, with its fine old pub The Chetham Arms, or uphill to Turton Heights and Chetham's Close.

Turton Tower has many 'boggart' stories including 'the silk-clad lady', as well as a boggart which later turned out to be a humble rodent, 'the lady with the long black skirt' and – most intriguing – 'the ghost at the bus stop'. This was reported on by the local press in 1954. Is the ghostly passenger still waiting? Given the infrequency of the buses nowadays, he could still be there.[112]

In the eighteenth century Turton Tower went into decline. However, in early Victorian times, its fortunes were revived when it was purchased by the successful inventor and entrepreneur James Kay in 1835. Kay had pioneered a 'wet spinning process' to enable flax to be spun more efficiently and produce a much finer and superior fabric. This gave a particular boost to production in Ireland, where the blue flowers of flax were a common sight until recent times. At the age of 61 he was able to retire, buy Turton Tower and pass the business on to his sons.

Kay did much to restore Turton Tower to its former glory, using oak panelling from Middleton Hall in parts of the building. My friend Professor Dick Horrocks has recently published a book on Kay, restoring him to his true importance in the history of the industrial revolution.[113]

By the early 1900s the hall was owned by Sir Lees Knowles, who occasionally hosted gatherings of the Lancashire Authors' Association (LAA) in the post-war period, which Clarke may well have attended. Knowles immersed himself in the

---

[111] *Moorlands* p. 210

[112] I am grateful to Dick Horrocks for much of the local information about Turton, including the boggarts!

[113] Richard Horrocks *James Kay of Turton Tower*, Bolton 2020

history of the building and gave detailed lectures to groups such as the LAA. [114]The tower is now managed by Blackburn with Darwen Council and owned by a trust; it features some fine historical displays and regular contemporary art exhibitions. There is a cafe which serves up good wholesome food for walkers and visitors.

Druids, giants and grand views

There's a choice of path from the Tower towards Entwistle. It's possible to cycle up the farm track, forming part of the 'Witton Weaver's Way', that runs on the west side of the railway past Clough House Farm and comes out on Green Arms Road. From there, you can cut across to Entwistle Reservoir.

Before you do though, stop off at the ornamental railway bridge just above the tower and walk up the staircase to the turret. Please give the train driver a friendly wave, you might get a toot back. The lovely bridge and its smaller sister just further up were provided by the railway company as a 'trade off' with the landowner to allow the construction of the line to go through the grounds. The small stone seat in the turret is a delightful touch.

The view from the 'turret' of Turton Tower Bridge

[114] See *The Record* November 1925 recording a meeting of the LAA at Turton Tower hosted by the Knowles's, and a report of Sir Lees Knowles' lecture on the history of Turton Tower. The association also met at the Tower on July 10th 1920, see *The Record* August 1920.

If you're on foot, it's a stiff but rewarding climb up to Chetham's Close, to the site of an ancient stone circle. Some maps show it as a 'Druidical Circle'. But who knows? Clarke says that the circle of seven stones was destroyed in 1892. He mentions the legend that *"these stones had been hurled across from Winter Hill, by a giant."*[115]

No smoking factory chimneys remain and the station has shut

Druids, giants, whatever. It's a fine panorama looking both to the west towards Winter Hill and east to Holcombe. We can at least partly agree with Clarke when he says: *"From these Turton Heights you have glorious views of the surrounding moorland and valleys – a grand view a hundred years ago, but rather marred in our day by the smoking factory chimneys of Blackburn and the Rossendale Valley."* [116]

It's interesting to reflect that a hundred years on, the smoking factories are no more - though to be honest you'd struggle to see chimneys in either Rossendale or Blackburn from where we're stood. But the immediate area was heavily industrialised. The local mills, including the adjacent towel mill, were served by the former Turton and Edgworth station which closed in 1961, a couple of years before the Beeching Axe came crashing down. Parts of the old platform remain. There has been a campaign to re-open it – a deserving project, given the residential development that has taken place nearby.

The station name was a misnomer: it's much nearer to Chapeltown than Edgworth village and 'Turton' is a generic name for this lovely area which covers a large expanse of moorland, farms and villages, half of the historic Turton being in Bolton and the other in Blackburn with Darwen. Only 'North' Turton has its own parish council, covering Belmont, Edgworth and Chapeltown. The historic Turton, cruelly divided by bureaucratic fiat, is served by the excellent Turton Local History Society which has a prolific output of publications, combined with regular meetings – in normal times.

The station goods yard survived longer than the passenger facility. The towel mill became a curtain net manufacturer into the 1970s though it had long ceased to have a siding connection. In Chapeltown village itself there was the larger 'Tower Mill'; some artefacts survive by the roadside. In 'Turton Bottoms' there was a very large mill complex, Vale Mill, which spun cotton yarns into the 1950s. Little of the mill settlement remains apart from some charming rows of workers' cottages and the manager's residence, Vale House.

---

[115] *Moorlands* p.213. The OS map shows it as 'Cheetham's Close'

[116] *Moorlands* p.213

Nearby is the site of Stone Mill which belonged to John Horrocks who lived at 'The Birches'; he cut and polished stone from local quarries. His younger son John erected some cotton spinning frames in his father's mill and built up his textile expertise. He moved to Preston about 1790 and founded what became the world-famous cotton enterprise of Horrocks and Co.

Sweet Harwood Lea

If you are planning a good day's walk, you could always 'take train' as Clarke would say, to Bromley Cross and walk via The Jumbles and over by Hardy Mill Quarry to Harwood, a little place of great charm, if only you look for it. Take the 507 bus back into Bolton.

I've already mentioned the poet and feminist Alice Collinge, who lived at 71 Riding Gate. Contemporary poet Stella Pye lives nearby and playwright Les Smith not far off; there is obviously something in the Harwood air that stimulates creativity. Another literary friend of Clarke's was James Windross, a Harwood man who was writing in the 1890s and early 1900s. He produced some fine poetry, mostly for *The Cotton Factory Times*, using a cotton industry non-de-plume of 'Roving'. The paper had a large circulation in the Lancashire textile districts before the First World War. For a short while in the late early 1890s Clarke worked for the paper, and continued to have his writing published in the *Factory Times* well into the 1920s.[117]

Riding Gate, Harwood, where Alice Collinge spent most of her later life. A 'flowery dell' of the sort that the poet James Windross missed so badly

[117] See Alan Fowler, Eddie Cass and Terry Wyke 'The remarkable rise and long decline of The Cotton Factory Times', Media History vol. 4 no. 2 1998

Windross was born and bred in Harwood but moved away; he obviously missed his native village. Clarke quotes his poem 'Harwood Lea', about home-sickness and loss.[118]

> *"Thy fair green fields, sweet Harwood Lea,*
> *Are incomparable to me;*
> *For here I spent my early days,*
> *When life was all a song of praise,*
> *Amid thy hills and flowery dells,*
> *Thy winding lanes and wayside wells."*

Harwood today has fewer 'flowery dells' but it still has some beautiful places that haven't been overwhelmed by suburban development. It also has some good independent shops, including the excellent green grocer which was able to keep going during the Lockdown.

Another view of Riding Gate showing Alice Collinge's former cottage, on left

[118] *Moorlands* p.258

16. Fair Entwistle and Enchanting Edgworth

"From Turton you can get amongst charming moorland scenery in all directions – on towards Entwistle (The railway viaduct between Turton and Entwistle is conspicuous, and not unpicturesque, for not all our modern works and devices are ugly and unromantic."[119]

Clarke doesn't say much about Entwistle but he admits to the beauties of the railway viaduct that crosses the Wayoh. When the reservoirs (Entwistle, and the lower Wayoh) were built, several buildings were simply flooded over and occasionally re-appear in defiance. He recalls seeing the tops of a farmhouse chimney after a very dry summer. I have similar memories of Wayoh in the 1970s.

Clarke always has a good eye for nature and wild flowers, and I like this description of the area, even if he gets his names confused – the quarry being 'Yarnsdale' not Earnsdale, near Tockholes:

"Then there is Earnsdale Quarry, with its bonny dingle and rocky gorge, and picturesque Armagreaves, with the bridge over the water connecting the two lakes near Entwistle. In May and June this moorland countryside is glorious with the golden flowers of the gorse, and many other fair wild flowers, including the dainty Wood Sorrel, and red Ragged Robin, and Marsh Marigolds delight the eye, while there are enchanting views of the valley and the hills."[120]

To me, Entwistle is the embodiment of what I love most about the moors. Part of its charm is that I've known it since boyhood. It's easily accessible by train with what is a rather basic station nowadays, a conveniently-located pub and walks fanning out in all directions. You can get a mix of woodland, open moors and waterside strolls within minutes of each other. And there's plenty to interest the industrial archaeologist.

Mills, mines and quarries

Like so much of these moors, the beauty of the landscape hides a gritty industrial past. Entwistle itself, until 1957, had a large factory – Know Mill – next to where the road drops down from Entwistle station. Most of it disappeared under the reservoir extension and it's hard to get any sense that it was once a busy place employing hundreds of workers. [121]

---

[119] *Moorlands* p.213

[120] *Moorlands* p.213. Usually spelt 'Yarnsdale' to distinguish it from Earnsdale Reservoir near Tockholes

[121] See the excellent village history *Entwistle* by Greg Walsh, published by Turton

A special train crosses Entwistle Viaduct, c 1983

Clarke has already referred to quarrying at Yarnsdale. There was much more, notably the large quarries at Round Barn near Whittlestone Head. A tramway linked the workings with the railway at Walton's Siding, close to the entrance to Sough Tunnel. An aerial ropeway, remains of which can be found if you search, ran down from the siding at Entwistle station to Know Mill. Further back in time, small coal mines littered the hills, such as those on Turton Moor, to the north-west of Entwistle.[122]

Up to Edgworth

If you're on a bike, it's a hard climb up from the Wayoh Reservoir along Hob Lane to the main road. It's also a narrow lane and many motorists get stuck with traffic coming up or down. At the top, there are some charming old cottages dating back to the 17th century. Turn left along the old Roman Road for Whittlestone Head and Blackburn, or right down to Edgworth. The village of Edgworth has expanded greatly since Clarke's day but it retains a strong sense of community.

The main focus of the village is The Barlow Institute, founded in 1909 by members of the Barlow family, Sir Thomas Barlow in particular, in memory of parents James and Alice. Thomas was born in nearby Brandwood Fold and was a physician to Queen Victoria.

Local History Society, 2011, for detailed accounts of the mill and its demise

[122] See Peter M. Harris *Mining in Turton*, Turton Local History Society, 2013

These days, 'The Barlow' is run by a trust. It has been working hard to raise funds for essential repairs. I hope they succeed – it's a great place which retains much of its original character. There are catering facilities downstairs in The Reading Room and a regular programme of cultural events. I very much hope that by the time you're reading this, it will be open for business once again.

James Barlow

Sir Thomas's father, James, was a remarkable man by any standards. He was the son of a handloom weaver, that group of mostly self-educated and intellectual working men who did so much for Lancashire culture, politics and industry. After a difficult start in life he went into quilt manufacture. By the 1880s he was a well-to-do business man involved in production of high quality cotton blankets, bedspreads and satin quilts and towels under the 'Osman' brand. His firm, Barlow and Jones, became world famous. He purchased a large estate above Edgworth and built the family home, 'Greenthorne'.

He developed numerous other business interests and found time to serve on Bolton Corporation in the 1860s and 1870s, representing Bradford Ward and then West Ward. He was a life-long temperance advocate and Methodist but doesn't seem to have been a prig. Whilst chairman of the Parks Committee he pressed for parks to open on Sundays. He was a strong supporter of the abolitionist cause during the American civil war.

Gandhi comes to visit

One of the most fascinating incidents in Turton history was the visit of Mahatma Gandhi to Edgworth in 1931. He was the guest of Annie Barlow, during his famous visit to Lancashire. The great man had been kept in prison by the British colonial authorities but was allowed out to travel to England and meet the cotton magnates with the hope that he might be persuaded to moderate his boycott of English cotton. He was entertained at the Barlow home and was greeted warmly by crowds of Lancashire cotton workers. Journalist Andrew Rosthorn wrote of the visit:

"In 1931 Annie Barlow invited Mahatma Gandhi to Edgworth. Britain had just been forced to leave the Gold Standard and one in every three cotton operatives was out of work, partly as a result of the boycott of Lancashire cotton in India in a mass movement championed by Mahatma Gandhi with his spinning wheel campaign. Gandhi was released from prison to travel to London for a round-table conference about the future of India. He took tea with the King and Queen when wearing his shawl and loin cloth. He also delighted a crowd of unemployed mill girls when his

train reached Spring Vale station outside Darwen late on Friday, September 25. On Saturday morning the over-protective police seemed surprised when he was welcomed by weavers at Greenfield Mill in Darwen. At 3:15 that afternoon the Mahatma arrived at Miss Barlow's isolated house at Edgworth for a secret meeting with the leaders of the textile industry."[123]

Gandhi's famous visit to Lancashire. The Mahatma is seen at Greenfield Mill, Darwen. *Photo courtesy Harold Heys*

He adds: *"Edgworth folk learned of the secret meeting before it was over. A crowd gathered. The police arrived to protect Gandhi, but the Mahatma was cheered on his way, to stay with some socialists and Quakers at West Bradford where he played some 'unbeatable' lawn tennis on the Sunday afternoon."*

The Children's Homes

Thomas Barlow cared passionately about the plight of children and gave land and a donation of £5000 to set up the Children's Homes at Crowthorn, above Edgworth, near to the family home. It opened in 1889. Clarke describes them as *"sweet and clean amid the rural beauty of the healthy moorlands."* He goes on to mention that *"these homes are kept going by public subscription, and, amongst other things, have a dairy which produces excellent cream for sale."* [124]

The home changed its role in 1953, becoming a school for children with special needs. It closed completely in 2002 and the site was sold for housing. Some of the

---

[123] I am indebted to Andrew Rosthorn for permission to use part of his article

[124] *Moorlands* p.214

buildings remain. The cream that Clarke extols is a distant memory but the little ice cream shop in the village centre is known for its excellent dairy ice cream and is always worth a call.

Down to Turton Bottoms

If you continue past The Barlow heading towards Bolton, look out for the weavers' cottages on both sides of the road, which rejoice in names such as 'Teapot Row', 'Kettle Row' and 'Grubb Street'. The road drops steeply down to Turton Bottoms, which as we've seen was once a busy industrial community with mills and print works. An attractive footpath takes you along the brook which emerges into The Jumbles and eventually leads to Bradshaw, or you can divert up to Bromley Cross station and get a train home.

Members of Edgworth Bowling Club enjoy September sunshine outside The Barlow. The Lancashire flag is flying!

17. Summer Evenings with Old Railwaymen

"In 1892 a new station building was in place complete with sidings. The station master, then Mr Richard Caldwell, was ably supported by ten staff. Mr Caldwell lived at the station master's house in the new Railway Terrace just behind Bridge House, the home of Mr William Horrocks, farmer and beer seller. This house was later named The Station Hotel, now the Strawbury Duck."[125]

Let's return to Entwistle - and a bit of self-indulgence - harking back to one of Allen Clarke's favourite books by a local author, James Swinglehurst. He wrote the short but delightful book *Summer Evenings with Old Weavers* in the 1880s. It reminded me of conversations I had back in the 1960s with two old railwaymen at Entwistle and Walton's Sidings signalboxes.

Entwistle is a very historic settlement, dating back to well before the Railway Age. But it became, to a degree, a railway community. The line, which crosses the attractive (even Allen Clarke admitted it!) Entwistle Viaduct, opened in 1848. It was constructed by the Bolton, Blackburn, Clitheroe and West Yorkshire Railway, which was absorbed by the Lancashire and Yorkshire Railway in 1858.

Building began in 1846 and progress was slow. Major works included the viaducts at Church Wharf and Tonge in Bolton, Entwistle Viaduct and, most challenging of all, the 2,015 yards long Sough Tunnel under Cranberry Moss. Five men were killed during its construction. The line finally opened in June 1848 with much celebration. [126]

The line climbed to a height of 737' feet at Whittlestone Head, where a temporary station was provided. It also had its own 'Railway Tavern', whose building remains as a private house. The signalbox was named Walton's Siding and handled traffic from the nearby quarry. Entwistle station was at first a relatively modest island platform connected to the road by a footbridge. In later years traffic expanded to the extent that new up and down 'through' lines were provided between Entwistle and Walton's Siding. At Entwistle goods traffic mainly served Know Mill in the valley below, linked by a rope-hauled tramway.

---

[125] Clive R. Walsh *Entwistle*, Turton Local History Society, 2011 p.93

[126] See W.D. Tattersall *The Bolton, Blackburn, Clitheroe and West Yorkshire Railway*, 1973, for a full and often entertaining account of the early history of the line

A view of Entwistle Station in Lancashire and Yorkshire Railway days.
Courtesy of L&Y Railway Society

Entwistle was a remote spot and the combination of goods and passenger traffic required a number of staff to be accommodated as close as possible to the station. The railway company constructed a row of brick houses – Railway Terrace - which still stand, just beyond the pub. When the L&YR built the 'relief' lines they provided a new signalbox which straddled the additional tracks on a gantry, offering good visibility of trains – and, as a bonus, some fine views of the surrounding landscape.

A railway community

Some of the houses in the surrounding area were occupied by railwaymen. Members of the Whitehead 'railway' family lived up Hob Lane. I remember David, now retired as a driver from Preston who served his time as a cleaner and fireman at Bolton. He was introduced to the girl who became his wife through the local signalman, Pat Hatzer (see below). His dad was Harry, a guard at Bolton. Family legend has it that the Whiteheads – dedicated railwaymen to their core – back in the 1920s would gather in one of their houses and spend the evening doing quiz games on the Railway Rule Book. Dedication indeed.

My first memories of Entwistle would be around 1965 when I cycled up from Great Lever on my new Dawes 'Don Juan' machine. It was a hard climb, especially up Batridge Road and Entwistle Hall Lane to the station. I watched a few trains go past then continued past the railway cottages and down to the reservoir, returning back through Chapeltown. It became a regular ride, usually with a camera to photograph the last of steam. The combination of a steep gradient and hard-working locomotives amidst fine scenery was a powerful attraction.

In the summer of 1966 I got to know the regular signalmen at both Entwistle and Walton's Siding. Pat Hatzer and Frank Carroll were the 'regular men' at Entwistle though at some point Frank moved 'up', at least in geographical terms, to Walton's. Both were very kind and friendly towards me, but they were as different as chalk and cheese and never really got on with each other. Interestingly, they were both from Catholic backgrounds, Pat being from a Polish family and Frank being Irish by origin. As a 'Thornleigh boy' in my mid-teens I was the acceptable face of train-spotting – or 'railway enthusiasm' as we preferred to call it.

Pat Hatzer and Frank Carroll

The Hatzers lived in Entwistle and Pat was part of a larger family, with children who have stayed in the area. I would either cycle up to Entwistle or catch the train, often with my friend Steve. We would climb up the signalbox steps to a warm welcome and cup of tea.

Those calm summer evenings were idyllic. By 1966 there were few steam-hauled freights over the route but two regular, heavily-loaded, trains ran in the evening. These were Brindle Heath (Salford) to Carlisle, usually followed about an hour later by the Ancoats – Carlisle. Whilst the 'Brindle Heath' could be anything from an LMS 'Black 5' to a 'Britannia' pacific, 'The Ancoats' was nearly always a Carlisle Kingmoor-based class 9F 2-10-0, the most powerful locos on BR by then.

In late June, if you were lucky, it was still light enough to photograph 'The Brindle Heath' but it was always dark by the time 'The Ancoats' came up. On occasion, you could hear it coming out of Bolton and hitting the climb past Astley Bridge Junction. It could be fifteen minutes before it stormed through Entwistle, but what a spectacle it made.

Inside a typical Lancashire and Yorkshire Railway signalbox (Windsor Bridge No. 3, Salford). Entwistle 'box was the same design, but smaller. Note the signalman's easychair! Every box had one

Of the two signalmen, Frank was the greater conversationalist. He would regale us with tales of his foreign travels using his BR passes, to places such as Constantinople, to inspect Byzantine treasures. He claimed to be from a strong Irish republican family with a father who had fought in the Dublin Easter Rising of 1916, alongside Patrick Pearse in the beleaguered GPO building. Whether he did or not I don't know but Frank could certainly tell a good tale.

When Frank moved to Walton's Siding box, possibly to escape from having to engage with Pat at the change of shift, his eccentricities became more pronounced. He lived in Collyhurst, a mile or so out of Manchester. Travelling to and fro was onerous and difficult so during the summer months he set up camp close to the signalbox and lived the life of a hermit. Another feature of Frank's time at Walton's Siding were his culinary habits. He would make a huge vat of soup at the beginning of the week and live off it until the weekend. When he was on nights, and traffic was light, he would nod off in his easychair and hope he would hear the 'call attention' bell from Entwistle box. After 'The Ancoats' had passed there was usually no other train until about 4.10 a.m. – the famous (in Bolton railway circles at any rate) 'Colne Papers'.

The Colne Papers

This legendary train took newspapers from Manchester to East Lancashire. It would load up on Manchester Victoria's Platform 11 Middle (the longest platform in the world), with consignments from the Manchester presses for Bolton, Darwen, Blackburn, Accrington, Burnley, Nelson and Colne. It departed on the dot at 3.45 a.m. For many years it was a Bolton 'job', with driver, fireman, guard and loco from Bolton. It was one of the shorter newspaper trains, compared with the heavy Glasgow and Newcastle trains, but it was very tightly timed. Bolton loco shed was very much a freight depot and the opportunities to run fast were limited to the occasional 'special' and 'The Colne Papers', usually pronounced 'Ceawn Papers' in Boltonese.

The first part of the job was in effect the 'tail end' of a working that entailed signing on mid-evening and working a parcels train from Bolton to Stockport. The loco then went to Red Bank carriage sidings to collect the four vans for the Colne train. At about 3.30 it would get the signal to drop down to Victoria to load up. The official timing to Bolton was 17 minutes, faster than most passenger trains, though it was a point of honour to do it in less. The train was allowed a few minutes at Bolton to change crews and unload the bundles of newspapers. The new crew – Bolton men again – took over for the run to Colne, returning 'light engine' to Bolton.

On a few occasions I rode on the footplate with the evening and early morning trip - the Stockport parcels and then from Victoria to Bolton. It was always a lively run and on occasions there were vociferous complaints from the sorting crew who were thrown around as the train took some of the pointwork at a higher speed than the rules permitted. Their ultimate sanction for too rough a ride run was to refuse the footplate crew their complimentary copies of the morning papers which would usually be distributed in the shed messroom.

Colonel Cut-off

One particular engineman who was noted for his fast-running was Bert Welsby, affectionately known as 'Colonel Cut-off' on account of his military bearing (with regimental-style 'tash') and his interest in the technicalities of locomotive valve gears. Sadly I never joined him for a ride on the Bolton to Colne part of the run – my parents wouldn't have looked kindly on me disappearing from home at 3 in the morning – but there are many stories of 'The Colonel' passing Walton's Siding in under eight minutes from Bolton, which would have involved an average speed of over 65 mph up a rising gradient of about 1 in 72. That's steep for a steam locomotive.

On one occasion, so legend has it, his progress was halted due to Frank's sleeping habits. The 'bobby' at Entwistle got the 'Papers' signalled from Turton box and sent the 'call attention' to Frank at Walton's. One beat of the bell; a loud 'ding'. No response. Another 'one' was sent and still no answer. The 'Papers' was steaming along nicely until Bert saw the 'distant' signal for Entwistle being 'on', meaning 'prepare to stop at the next signal'. The signalman went down to the track to inform Bert that he couldn't get 'line clear' from Walton's Siding and he'd have to wait. Meanwhile, newsagents throughout East Lancashire were expecting their newspaper delivery. Eventually, the signalman was roused from his dreams and he gave 'line clear' and pulled off his signals to let the train on its way.

Where are they now? Frank will be up there driving the angels mad with his tales. Pat will be looking askance, 'that flaming Carroll again!' Of both it can be said, we shall not see their like again.

18. Steaming into 'Rammy' and Rawtenstall

"Most parts of Rossendale I have skimmed through on the cycle, and from the high moorland road, have judged what a beautiful valley it must have been once upon a time, and is still fair." [127]

Clarke loved Rossendale. He writes about it affectionately in *Moorlands and Memories*, though there's a qualification in the above praise, wouldn't you say? When Clarke was writing, Rossendale, or at least the core valley between Rawtenstall and Bacup, was a bustling, but polluted, industrial powerhouse. Rossendale led the world in slipper manufacture, as well as having a thriving textile industry, with coal-mining and quarrying. Handloom-weaving was slow to die out in the small farmsteads and folds up in the hills. These communities produced many talented individuals, as we shall see, and there was a strong culture that permeated the valley based on music and literature as well as botany and geology.

Many examples of this deep-rooted culture have been preserved at the excellent Whitaker Museum and Art Gallery in Rawtenstall. Further up the valley, Bacup Natural History Society is still alive and well in its long-established home on the Todmorden Road.

Railways of Rossendale

Despite the hilly terrain, Rossendale developed a good rail network, with the added bonus of trams running through the valley from Bacup to Rawtenstall with a branch to Water.

It wasn't to last. The trams went in the early 1930s. The railways of Rossendale fared badly under Dr Beeching, just as the mills were closing. Rossendale suffered what some economists have called 'structural disinvestment', i.e. the whole area was hammered with both jobs and infrastructure disappearing. The line from Rochdale to Bacup, over the magnificent Healey Dell Viaduct, had closed to passenger traffic as early as 1947. The busy route from Bury via Ramsbotton ('Rammy') and Rawtenstall to Bacup was shut in December 1966. It survived with a limited passenger service to Rawtenstall until 1972, though freight traffic continued with a monthly coal train until the early 1980s.

I hitched a ride on that train when I was working for the British Rail Property Board back in 1978; I had been sent to inspect the level crossing at Townsend Fold. I was lucky to find the coal train, with a 'class 40' diesel at its head, sat in the

---

[127] *Moorlands* p.263

platform at Bury Bolton Street station. I showed my BR pass and the driver kindly allowed me into the cab.

I soon realised he had an agenda though. When we stopped at Ramsbottom to get the 'token' for the next stretch of the single line he told me to jump out and get a couple of meat pies from the bakers' just up the road. This completely disrupted traffic on the road and it wasn't helped by a large queue at the pie shop. I managed to jump to the head of the throng by explaining that I was on a train that was blocking the road. The unbelieving proprietor popped his head out of the door and realised I was telling the truth. I got the pies and we continued our way up the branch.

The Famous 4.25

The former 'main line' to East Lancashire, which thrust northward from Stubbins Junction (just north of Ramsbottom) to Accrington was an important route from Manchester to the thriving industrial towns of Accrington, Burnley, Nelson and Colne. One of the most famous trains to grace the Lancashire and Yorkshire Railway was the iconic 4.25 pm Salford to Colne, one of the early L&Y 'commuter' trains, consisting of 10 coaches, mostly occupied by first class season ticket holders whose business would have been on the Manchester Cotton Exchange (Th'Change), which was easily walkable from Salford station.

The train ran non-stop to Burnley Barracks, but 'slipped' a coach whilst sneaking round the tight curve at Accrington. The running time from Salford to Burnley was 49 minutes, which I suspect you would struggle to achieve that by any form of transport today. The train was entrusted to nothing bigger than one of Aspinall's sturdy 2-4-2 'Radial Tanks' built at Horwich from the 1880s. It was Agecroft shed's no. 1 'job' and was often entrusted to the care of the redoubtable Driver Shorrock who knew how to extract every ounce of power out of his engine up the steep gradients from Clifton Junction and then north of Bury.

Eric Mason, shedmaster at Agecroft for many years and author of *The Lancashire and Yorkshire Railway in the 20th Century*, described Shorrock as "*one of the most skilful exponents of engine management of his day*". He also called the route of the 4.25 as "*one of the most difficult lengths of railway in the country,*" climbing to a height of 771 ft. at Baxenden and then dropping at a 1 in 44 gradient to Accrington, where drivers had to negotiate the 5 mph slack round the curve onto the 'main line' to Rose Grove. The 4.25 featured in the columns of *The Railway Magazine* during 1922, with the eminent author and train-timer Cecil J. Allen waxing lyrical at Shorrock's exploits.[128]

---

[128] See C. J. Allen in *The Railway Magazine* December 1922

Re-birth of a railway

After closure of the Bacup and Baxenden lines, Rossendale was saddled with the unhappy distinction of being the only borough in Lancashire without a railway. However, there has been a re-birth of sorts. After an attempt by preservationists to re-open parts of the Stubbins to Accrington section foundered, plans to re-open from Bury to Rawtenstall went forward after the coal traffic finished in December 1980. On July 25th 1987 the first train ran from Bury to Ramsbottom, to great rejoicing. The East Lancashire Railway reached Rawtenstall in April 1991 and Heywood in 2003.

A 'Jinty' loco at a revived Ramsbottom station in 2018

The possibility of getting beyond Rawtenstall to Bacup seems remote; part of the line has been built on and some of it now forms a road. But who knows? An easier option would be to extend the Heywood line into Castleton, providing a link to the national passenger network. A proposal to provide a regular passenger service from Bury to Rochdale has been made to the Government's rail re-openings fund. There's also suggestions of the Bury (or Radcliffe) to Bolton route being converted to Metrolink tram operation.

For now, the East Lancashire Railway has a huge job on its hands recovering from the hammer blows of the coronavirus crisis. Services were suspended in March 2020, just when the railway was gearing up for a busy Easter weekend which would lead on to the summer season. Services re-commenced in late July on a reduced basis. The message must surely be, don't let history repeat itself and see this valuable part of Lancashire's history – and visitor economy – disappear.

19. Rossendale Radicals and Reformers

"Thomas Newbigging, the writer of our chief local classic, the 'History of the Forest of Rosendale', is no more! He has, at the age of 81 years, faded out from earthly life and passed to a higher sphere. But his works do follow him."[129]

Thomas Newbigging

The Rossendale Valley has produced some remarkably talented writers and politicians and none more so than Thomas Newbigging, in many ways the personification of the Northern radical Liberal tradition. He was one of Lancashire's most respected figures in the 1870s and 1880s, a champion of Irish freedom and a strong democrat. Newbigging provides a link from Owenism through Liberalism towards Socialism. [130] Allen Clarke often referred to his writings, particularly his magnificent *History of the Forest of Rossendale.*[131]

Of Scots Presbyterian origins, Newbigging was born in Glasgow in 1833. His parents had been brought up and educated in New Lanark, Robert Owen's socialist community to the south of Glasgow, where they had met and married. They then settled in Glasgow in the early 1830s, when his father was appointed manager of a large cotton mill. After some years in Galloway the family moved to Lancashire in 1844.

At the age of twenty-three Newbigging was appointed manager of the Rossendale Union Gas Company, based in Bacup at the head of the Rossendale Valley. He went on to become one of Britain's leading gas engineers, spending some years in Brazil. He wrote the standard text for the gas industry, *The Gas Manager's Handbook*, published in 1881.

Thomas Newbigging

It was his extensive non-professional interests that mark Newbigging out as exceptional. He was author of *The History of the Forest of Rossendale*, a work which has yet to be surpassed for its detailed historical description of the area. He was also a talented poet, strongly influenced by Burns; his *Poems and Songs* combine traces of

[129] Obituary by Samuel Compston in *Rossendale Free Press*, June 6th 1914

[130] See Paul Salveson *Socialism with a Northern Accent*, 2012

[131] Thomas Newbigging *History of the Forest of Rossendale*, 1868

both Lancashire and Scots vernacular. Like many middle-class intellectuals of his day he was fascinated by dialect and, with Henry Cunliffe, wrote a *Glossary of Rochdale-cum-Rossendale Words and Phrases*. He was a member of the Manchester Literary Club and many other literary circles and was a good friend of the famous Lancashire dialect poet Edwin Waugh.[132]

Newbigging's parental background seems to have instilled a strong social awareness in him. His politics were Liberal, on its radical edge. In 1886 he was adopted as the Liberal 'Home Rule' candidate for Rossendale; six verbatim reports of his election speeches were published in 1887. Whilst not a great deal has been written about Newbigging, the collection of his political speeches, including the six from the 1886 contest and a further twelve from the rest of 1886 and from 1887, are important documents of political history. The speeches were mostly given in Rossendale, though some were made in other locations across Lancashire and Yorkshire, including Salford, Manchester and Huddersfield.

The main theme of the election speeches was Ireland. The issue of home rule for Ireland dominated the 1886 election and split the Liberal Party between unionists and followers of Gladstone who wanted some measure of self-government for Ireland. Newbigging was a passionate believer in Irish freedom, seeing Home Rule as a stepping stone to complete national independence. He was a strong supporter and ally of fellow Rossendalian Michael Davitt (see below).

At a speech in the Public Hall, Haslingden, Newbigging paid tribute to the leader of the Irish Land League as *"a man of unblemished character, and his nobility of soul is recognised by friend and foe alike."* In another speech in Eccles he again returned to the Irish Question, observing that *"the history of Ireland and its connection with England, both before and since the Act of Union ... is indeed such as to make even a heart of stone bleed."*[133]

In response to accusations that Davitt and other Irish radicals were 'demagogues and agitators' he cited the English radical tradition: *"We owe every shred of our English liberty to men who were called demagogues and agitators, and viler names than these ... the truth is we need more agitators"*. He attacked Tory attempts to 'play the Orange card', and accused Randolph Churchill of *"opening wide the door of race and religious bigotry."*

Newbigging was passionate about religious equality, land reform, free education for all and strong local government. He was also an early advocate of devolution

---

[132] For Waugh and the Manchester Literary Club, see Martha Vicinus, *Edwin Waugh: the ambiguities of self-help*, 1984

[133] Thomas Newbigging, *Speeches and Addresses*, Bacup 1887, p.71

for Scotland, Wales and England, as well as Ireland, objecting to 'the unwieldy growth of London', which he saw as sapping talent from the rest of the country. His speech at Failsworth during the 1886 election campaign highlighted the dangerously centralised government in Britain:

"...there is a magnetic force of attraction towards the governmental centre of the country. Talent, genius, the possessors of great wealth, the victims of poverty – all converge towards the central core of the nation's life; and when, as in the case of London, the growth becomes stupendous almost beyond conception, there is grave reason for apprehension."[134]

If he thought it was bad then!

He lost the election, quite narrowly, to the well-known Liberal 'Unionist' Lord Hartington. But his legacy endures more than that of his successful rival. Newbigging was a central figure in the Lancashire dialect movement, a talented creative writer and historian as well as being an internationally-respected gas engineer. A unique combination, without any doubt. He died in 1914.

Michael Davitt

"You know Michael Davitt. He was reared in your midst; in this very town he grew from youth to manhood. I think he must have imbibed many of his idea of freedom in breathing the air of the Rossendale hills." – Thomas Newbigging, speaking in Haslingden [135]

Michael Davitt was one of the outstanding figures in Irish and indeed British politics in the late 19th century. He was founder of the Irish Land League and did perhaps more than anyone to end landlordism in Ireland and pave the way for Irish independence. He was a revered figure in Lancashire's Irish community, which Clarke was born into; his father and grandfather both had strong 'Fenian' sympathies and in his later life Clarke spoke passionately about James Connolly, the great socialist and republican who was executed for his part in Dublin's Easter Rising of 1916.

The story of Michael Davitt, honoured as a national hero in Ireland but virtually forgotten in Britain, personifies the course of Irish radicalism in the North of England in the second half of the nineteenth century. Davitt's family were evicted from their cottage in Straide, Co. Mayo, during the Potato Famine in 1850. They landed at Liverpool and settled in Haslingden. They lived in the town's 'Little

---

[134] *Speeches and Addresses* p.223

[135] *Speeches and Addresses*, p.24

Ireland' and the family became part of the rapidly growing Lancashire Irish community.

Michael Davitt

Davitt went to work in a local mill at the age of nine but lost his arm in one of the frequent accidents which befell children working in a dangerous industrial environment. This may have been a blessing in disguise, since he was taken under the wing of the local postmaster, Henry Cockroft, and gained what would have been a good education for a working class child of his time.

By the mid-1860s, the younger members of the Irish community in towns like Haslingden were increasingly drawn to the Fenian movement and established secret local groups which were dedicated to achieving Irish freedom by any means necessary. Davitt became the leader of the Rossendale 'centre' and was soon appointed organiser for Scotland and the North of England, becoming involved in arms smuggling activities.

The ability to access firearms proved useful when anti-Catholic mobs attacked local churches. In 1868, Davitt led the defence of St Mary's church in Haslingden; he and a small group of fellow Fenians fired above the heads of the approaching mob which quickly dispersed.

After living the life of an underground revolutionary, Davitt was eventually arrested and sentenced to a heavy term of imprisonment, serving much of his time in the hell-hole that was Dartmoor. When he came out of jail he turned from the politics of Fenianism to non-violent campaigns for land reform. The most burning issue in rural Ireland was landlordism and the inhuman treatment of the peasantry.

The Irish 'Land Wars' of the late 1870s and early 1880s culminated in a remarkable victory for Davitt and the Irish Land League, after facing mass evictions and savage repression by a police force who sided with the landlords. Davitt developed the policy of 'passive resistance' which directly inspired Gandhi. It proved successful, with legislation passed during the 1880s which gave a large degree of security to Ireland's rural workers.

Much of Davitt's campaigning took place outside of Ireland. He travelled extensively across the United States as well as Britain. There is a plaque on the side of the Portree Hotel, Skye, commemorating his visit to the island during the Crofters' struggle for land rights in 1887. Actually there are two plaques, one in Gaelic, t'other English. Davitt spoke with a strong Lancashire accent and was fluent in Irish (the family language) as well as English. I wonder if he addressed the thousands of assembled Sgiathanach (Skye folk) in Irish or Scots Gaelic, English or Lanky?

He was hugely popular in the North of England, idolised by the Irish community but widely respected amongst liberals and socialists alike. The experience of prison had a terrible effect on his health and he died at the age 60, in 1906. If forgotten by mainstream English politics, he is remembered by the Lancashire Irish community and revered 'wherever green is worn'.

In his home town of Haslingden 'The Land League Club' or - to use its correct title - the Irish Democratic League Club - survives. It's tucked away on George Street. Nearby is a memorial garden with a plaque which reads: *"This memorial has been erected to perpetuate the memory of Michael Davitt with the town of Haslingden. It marks the site of the home of Michael Davitt, Irish patriot, who resided in Haslingden from 1853 to 1867. He became a great world figure in the cause of freedom and raised his voice and pen on behalf of the oppressed, irrespective of race or creed, that serfdom be transformed to citizenship and that man be given the opportunity to display his God-given talents for the betterment of mankind. Born 1846, died 1906. Erected by the Irish Democratic League Club, Haslingden (Davitt Branch)."*

Samuel Compston

Rossendale had a strong Liberal tradition, exemplified by figures such as Thomas Newbigging, a 'comer-in' from Scotland as we've seen. Another Liberal politician who spent much of his long life in Rossendale was Samuel Compston, who was devoted to his community's history and culture. He was born in Radcliffe in 1842 and the family then moved to Rochdale and later to Bradford. They lived in Settle between 1855 and 1867 where his father was a Congregational minister. He seems to have moved to Rossendale in the late 1870s and settled in Crawshawbooth where he lived up to his death in 1933 at the age of 91. [136]

He was a man of varied interests. His obituary in the Lancashire Authors' Association *Record* notes that he was *"a voluminous contributor to the newspaper press"* and also wrote many books and pamphlets on subjects as varied as *Alcohol*

[136] See short biography in *The Record* August 1916 and his obituary in the March 1934 edition

Compston Cross on the moors above Goodshaw

and the Nervous System, The History of Ewood Dale and *Quakerism in Rochdale*. He wrote the classic account of the 'Deighn Layrocks' (see next chapter) and was an authority of Lancashire dialect. He was a JP and served on Rawtenstall Borough Council for 43 years. He was a Quaker, with the radical and liberal views that went with it, being actively involved in the historic Friends meeting house in his home village of Crawshawbooth. He was a committed advocate of the temperance cause and lectured for the British Temperance Society, for whom he was 'scientific adviser'.

He gave a fascinating paper to the Lancashire Authors' Association meeting in Rawtenstall in 1930, on 'Rossendale and Rossendale Folk'. The talk was wide-ranging and he praised Rossendale people as 'shrewd, freedom-loving and generally commendable'. [137]He went on to mention the role of the Co-operative movement and its origins in Rochdale. As a young man he used the extensive Co-operative Society library. He wrote a series of important articles for *The Rossendale Free Press* on the remarkable musical accomplishments of the handloom-weaving communities of Rossendale (see next chapter).

---

137 *The Record*, September 1930

He was a member of the Lancashire Authors' Association from 1916 and would have rubbed shoulders with Allen Clarke on many occasions; he was vice-president for a number of years. *The Record* notes that *"as a public representative he helped to preserve for the people several moorland paths threatened with closure, including that to Waugh's Well."* [138]

Samuel Compston

In 1902 the historic cross on the moors above Crawshawbooth – now part of The Rossendale Way – was re-built, largely thanks to the efforts of Compston. The opening ceremony was attended by a large gathering of people, including Newbigging and Compston himself. At some point it became known as 'Compston's Cross' and so it should be. The views from the cross, looking down to Clowbridge reservoir and beyond to Longridge Fell, are spectacular.

In 1996 the cross was once again re-built though the lettering on it is now badly faded. But everyone seems to know it as 'Compston's Cross'. The old radical has a street named after him in his village of Crawshawbooth, a few yards down from Goodshaw Chapel where the 'Deighn Layrocks' often performed. Who? Read on.....

---

[138] *The Record*, March 1934. Waugh's Well commemorates the great dialect poet Edwin Waugh – see Chapter 25

20. Up with the Larks: The Choral Tradition of Rossendale

" The inhabitants of the Dean valley have long been celebrated for their excellence as musicians, both vocal and instrumental; and it is from this fact that their appellation of 'Deyghn Layrocks' has arisen. From records more than a century and a half old we learn that they were in the habit of meeting in each other's houses by turns, and practising the compositions, sacred and secular, which our country can boast in such rich abundance." [139]

One of Lancashire's finest gifts to the world is its musical tradition. While it is rightly proud of towering figures such as Blackburn's Kathleen Ferrier and St Helens' Thomas Beecham, there is a tradition of community-based music-making which reached its apogee in one of the small tributary valleys in Rossendale. The story of 'The Larks of Dean' – or 'Deighn Layrocks – is one of the most fascinating tales in Lancashire's cultural history, though is perhaps little known a hundred years on since Allen Clarke praised – almost in passing – the village of Dean, *"noted for its singing – its inhabitants being known as 'Deighn Layrocks (larks)."* [140]

The Larks of Dean couldn't sleep before a concert! An early cartoon showing father and son rehearsing in the middle of the night. From Newbigging's *Lancashire Humour* , 1900

So let's unravel this story a bit further. Two of our 'Rossendale radicals' mentioned in the previous chapter, Newbigging and Compston, extolled the achievements of these remarkable musicians, mostly handloom weavers. In more recent times, Roger Elbourne in his *Music and Tradition in Early 19th Century Lancashire,* uses the research of Compston in particular to bring the story of 'Th'Deighn

---

[139] *History of the Forest of Rossendale* pp.191-2

[140] *Moorlands* p.262

Layrocks' to a modern audience. [141]

A venerable race...

Thomas Newbigging wrote about 'The Larks of Dean' in his *History of the Forest of Rossendale*, published in 1868. The text was re-published in his *Sketches and Tales* in 1883 and in *Lancashire Characters and Places* in 1891. He mentions the diary of Sir Ralph Assheton 'a hospitable Lancashire baronet of the 17th century' who records donating the sum of 10s to 'The Rossendale players', demonstrating the longevity of music-making in Rossendale, describing its exponents as *"a venerable race, and can count their congeners back through the centuries."*[142]

Newbigging goes on to identify the tiny handloom-weaving communities in the Rossendale hills as centres of musicianship, both sacred and secular. He had a manuscript collection of over 50 'psalm tunes and chants' that were composed by the musicians of the Dean Valley and other parts of Rossendale, but believed it was only a fraction of the total opus.

He says *"Numerous are the stories that are told of the modes in which the enthusiasm of the 'Layrocks' is or was displayed in their pursuit of the musical art. In handloom days, when every man's house was his workshop, it was usual for the Deyghners to repair to each other's houses alternately, after the Sunday service at the chapel, and continue their practice of music far into the small hours of the Monday morning."* Compositions included titles such as 'Happy Simeon', 'Bocking Warp', 'Strong Samson', 'Old Methuselah' and 'Spanking Rodger'. [143]

Glorious choruses

As well as their own compositions, the 'layrocks' were passionate about the works of the great composers of the day, immersing themselves, as Newbigging wrote, in *"the glorious choruses of Handel and Haydn, the melting melodies of Beethoven and Mendelssohn."*[144]

Edwin Waugh, whom we will meet later, describes meeting the 'layrocks' whilst rambling across the Rossendale moors 'over the heathery waste of Swinshaw

---

[141] Roger Elbourne *Music and Tradition in Early 19th Century Lancashire 1780 -1840*, Folklore Society, 1980. See also the excellent article by Jean Seymour (leader of the Larks of Dean Quire) on the website of the West Gallery Music Association http://www.wgma.org.uk/Articles/Larks/article.htm

[142] Thomas Newbigging *History of the Forest of Rossendale*, Bacup 1883. Note that the dialect version of 'Dean' has various spellings, but 'Deighn' is the most common

[143] *History of the Forest of Rossendale* p.192

[144] *History of the Forest of Rossendale* p.191

towards Dean'. He met a crowd of people coming towards him, many of whom were carrying musical instruments. At his request, the assembled entourage gave a stirring impromptu performance for the poet, with Waugh recollecting that *"they played and sang several fine pieces of psalmody upon the heather-scented mountain top."*[145]

Newbigging himself describes attending a performance at Lumb Chapel, probably in the mid-1860s, as part of 'field day' celebrations. He notes that *"The Singers' Chapel was thronged to excess. In the forefront was a dazzling row of buxom girls, with ruddy faces and sparkling eyes, the picture of that rosy health which the fresh and bracing air of the hillside imparts...behind the girls were the males of every age, from the youthful tyro to the hoary and spectacled patriarchs of the valley; and in the rear were the instrumentalists, among whom the fiddlers, large and small predominated. The mellow flute and the clarionet had their representatives; and dotted here and there, might be seen a brass instrument, reflecting the bright sunshine that gleamed through the windows of the humble edifice."*[146]

A cello – made and played by one of 'The Larks' - in The Whitaker Museum, Rawtenstall

The performance began with a rendition of 'Nativity' but the grand finale was the 'Hallelujah Chorus', with the choir and entire congregation joining in with great enthusiasm.

The tradition of the Deighn Layrocks survived the end of handloom-weaving in the valley. This was a long drawn-out process but the great days of handloom weaving had come to an end by the 1840s, with just a few 'patriarchs' remaining at the loom, weaving some of the fancier cloths. Samuel Compston devoted much time and effort to researching the history of the 'Deighn Layrocks', making extensive use of the diary of one of their number, Moses Heap of Crawshawbooth.[147]

Elbourne quotes the modern Rossendale historian Chris Aspin who stressed that despite the transition from handloom weaving to

---

[145] Edwin Waugh 'An Incident by the Wayside' *Home Life of the Lancashire Factory Folk during the Cotton Famine*, 1863 pp.199-200

[146] *History of the Forest of Rossendale* p.193

[147] Moses Heap, *My Life and Times* (microfilm in Manchester Central Library). No date but poss. 1890s

factory work, this does not seem to have impacted on the musical life of the Dean workers. *"Heap first took singing lessons at Goodshaw when he was 15 and working more than 70 hours a week in a mill. Forty others attended the class in the tiny hamlet."*[148]

Compston published a series of articles on The Deighn Layrocks in the *Rossendale Free Press* between September 17th 1904 and January 7th 1905 which are included in Elbourne's book as an appendix.

Whilst the music-making had its epi-centre in Dean, there was strong musical activity nearby villages including Loveclough, Goodshaw and Lumb. A feature of the music-making in Rossendale was that many of the musical instruments were made by the musicians themselves. Some of these are kept at the Whitaker Museum in Rawtenstall, including a very large 'serpent' wind instrument, clarinet and fiddle.[149] Compston describes an old French violin which had probably been bought second-hand by one of the 'Layrocks' "but must have been good enough to satisfy the taste of 'Dick o'James's". He then adds *"But Deighn could make its own fiddles if it wanted. James Ashworth...the son of Old Bob "t'Carr, is said to have made a fiddle out of a tub lag, i.e. from one of the pieces of wood or legs of which a cask is formed when all are bound round by loops.."*[150]

Compston identifies the fiddle-maker 'par-excellence' as James Nuttall, of Spring Gardens, Dean, whom he describes as *"an adept all-round worker in wood"* who could make shuttles and pickers for hand-looms, as well as many other wooden items of domestic use, including coffin lids![151]

The female larks

An important part of the Layrocks' story was the active involvement of women. We have already heard Newbigging's slightly racy description of the choir girls at Lumb Chapel. However, many older women played an active and equal part in the choral singing, including Sally and Nelly Nuttall. Sally Nuttall was the last of the line of female 'Layrocks' who died age 87 in 1903. She described to Compston walking over the moors at night-time to attend concerts in neighbouring villages, with only a hand-made lantern to guide them. They often arrived at Goodshaw Chapel soaked through and had to take off their clogs and wring out their stockings which

---

[148] Chris Aspin *Lancashire, the First Industrial Society*, 1969, p.171

[149] Some of the hymn books are kept at The Whitaker, with a larger collection in the Lancashire County Archives in Preston

[150] *Music and Tradition in Industrial Lancashire* p.126

[151] *Music and Tradition in Industrial Lancashire* p.127, from *Rossendale Free Press* October 29th 1904

had got saturated in the boggy moorland.[152]

The tradition continues

There is a 'Larks of Dean Quire' based in Bury. Across East Lancashire the choral tradition is alive and well, with an East Lancashire Clarion Choir continuing the longstanding links with the socialist movement. Bolton also has its own Clarion Choir which has taken to doing open-air impromptu concerts in Queen's Park during the coronavirus restrictions.

East Lancashire Clarion Choir in rehearsal outside Clarion House

[152] *Music and Tradition in Industrial Lancashire* p.129

21. Mist and rain over Pendle and tea at Clarion House

"Clarion House is an important part of our working class history. The vision that drove those early socialist pioneers to build The Clarion, set as it is in the beautiful open countryside, so that working people could escape the mills and factories and enjoy their small amount of free time, should not be forgotten."[153]

A wet day out

Clarke was very fond of Pendle and frequently cycled out to the 'foothills' around Barley and Roughlee. He had friends in Burnley, including Tom Booth the town's librarian, the rambler Joe Bates ('Boshemengro'), poet Henry Houlding and John Allen, secretary of Burnley's Literary Society. It was a long ride from Bolton and occasionally he resorted to train travel, leaving his faithful bike at home or loading it in the guard's van. He describes one occasion when he 'took train' to Todmorden and on to Burnley where he met Joe Bates. Pendle was shrouded in mist and before long it began to rain heavily. But the downpour eventually stopped, allowing him and Joe Bates to head for Barley:

"a pleasant walk, of which I retain memories of grand chestnut trees in their white loveliness, the charming mauve of the lilac, the blossom of orchards, wayside pansies, and a sight of bonny birds by Pendle Water."[154]

A ride through fairest scenery

They never got to the summit of Pendle – the mist was still down and they were warned by a friendly 'bobby' of dangers of getting lost 'on the tops'. Clarke vowed to return another day and a few days later – Whitsuntide – he and his wife once again took train', this time to Blackburn and then cycled through Whalley, Clitheroe and on to Gisburn. He writes:

"After passing through Clitheroe we saw the happy spectacle of Whitsuntide filled-days – the white dresses of the maidens looking pretty against the green surroundings. Bands were playing, young men and maids were enjoying 'kiss in the ring' and other games, and all the world seemed given to Arcadian festivity." [155]

---

[153] Sue Nike, chair of ILP Land Society and Clarion House volunteer, in Introduction to *The Last Clarion House*, 2018

[154] *Moorlands* p.225

[155] *Moorlands* p.226

The enjoyed *"a glorious ride through fairest scenery, trees, wild flowers, Pendle Hill on one side of the valley and Longridge Fells on the other,"* until reaching Gisburn, where they went down to the Ribble, enjoying a woodland idyll amidst cherry trees, more lilac and blossom. I wonder if they took 'the back road' via Sawley Abbey and Bolton-by-Bowland, still a pleasant and quiet route compared to the horrors of the A59.

Between 1962 and 1994 you wouldn't have been able to 'take train to Clitheroe'. The station re-opened for occasional 'DalesRail' specials in the 1970s and this is a view from the cab of the very first train to use the new station in 1975. Regular services commenced nearly 20 years later

He records having lunch in The White Bull at Gisburn – an unusual reference to local hostelries – and then riding back to Chatburn from where they planned to get the train home. At the station they were greeted with a remarkably 'Whitmanesque' scene. *"The railway station was full of holiday-makers, everyone carrying a great bunch of lilac. The folks looked like walking gardens."* [156]

A fascinating and delightful image! Was this an annual tradition of going to the Ribble Valley and collecting lilac? The florally-clad folk are clearly not local – he describes them as 'holiday-makers' and they are obviously waiting to get the same train home as the Clarkes.

[156] *Moorlands* p.227

Gathering of the scribes and ramblers

He describes a further visit to Pendle when he and Lila actually reached the top, pushing their bikes up from Barley. Although he doesn't give a date – probably late 1890s – it was a special event:

"There was a gathering there that day of Northern Weekly rambling clubs from all parts of the shire – Boshemengro and his contingent, Rachda Rambler and his friends, old philosophic Aspinall and galvanic Grunshaw, and the rhyming Sarah Ann Robinson and their group from Padiham, and many others – it was a sight to see – and a treat to hear, the crowd on the top of the hill singing nature songs and hymns."[157]

Writing a few years later, as 'Capanbells', he reminisces about that day, following the arrival of a bunch of heather sent by his friend Joe Bates:

"I remember Pendle,
Where in days gone by
Crowds of comrades gathered
'Neath the moor top sky;
Oh the friendly greetings,
When our hearts were jolly bowls
With fellowship o'er flowing,
And the vision in our souls!"[158]

We shall return to Clarke's network of rambling and cycling clubs in a later chapter. He was adept at creating strong, informal networks – even in his 60s he set up the Blackpool Ramble Club which became one of the largest in the country. The friends he mentions at the Pendle meeting were an interesting bunch. I've already introduced 'Boshemengro' (Joe Bates). 'Rachda Rambler' was his friend A.W. Webster who often wrote for *Northern Weekly*. Sarah Ann Robinson was the daughter of 'galvanic Grunshaw' who had been involved in the Chartist movement back in the 1840s. Sarah was a weaver and a talented poet.

Clarke's love for Pendle was developed in one of his most interesting novels, *The Red Flag*, published in 1908 by The Twentieth Century Press, the publishing house of the Social Democratic Federation (SDF). It was first serialised in his short-lived newspaper *Teddy Ashton's Weekly*, the continuation of *Northern Weekly*, from 1907-8.

---

[157] *Moorlands* p.228

[158] 'Pendle Hill' in *Teddy Ashton's Lancashire Annual*, 1908

Unlike most of Clarke's novels, it is overtly political. It includes classic Allen Clarke 'melodrama' with heroes and villains and the couple who, despite all the obstacles, come together and live happily ever after. Some historical figures have 'walk-on' parts including Mary Higgs of Oldham, who was an acquaintance of Clarke's. She was from a fairly prosperous middle class background but 'went on the tramp' to see what life was really like for the 'bottom dogs' of society.

The Great Meeting

One of the most memorable scenes in the novel is 'the great meeting' on the top of Pendle, no doubt inspired by his *Northern Weekly* gathering, most of whose participants would have been part of the emerging socialist movement that was so strong in North-east Lancashire. Clarke despaired of the rival factions within the socialist movement, particularly the split between the more 'ethical socialist' Independent Labour Party and the Marxist-oriented SDF. In the novel, the lovers are, respectively, members of the ILP and SDF. With all-too-obvious metaphorical flourish, they seal their love on the top of Pendle, as the banners of the ILP and SDF come together in political unity.

They meet at Burnley ('Brunborough') station and make the long walk up to Pendle through the town's terraced streets then out into the countryside. At the top of Pendle they are met by a large throng of men and women. Collectively, they represent the flower of Lancashire socialism in its heroic phase. Clarke's description of them is deeply moving:

An ILP family walk c 1900. Getting out into the surrounding countryside was an essential part of early socialist culture

"They were mostly of the working class – weavers, spinners, joiners, miners, engineers, mechanics, though there were a few shopkeepers, clerks, journalists and doctors amongst them. All were

full of good humour – joking, laughing, chatting of past meetings and doings...All were dressed in their best, though some were pathetically shabby; their garb, their faces, told of the struggle in which they toiled; but their eyes were alight with the hope of the good time coming – the good time of justice and fair play for all – the time they were bringing nearer by this enthusiastic gathering, to proclaim once more the message they were spreading throughout the land, the gospel of salvation for the shorn and enslaved. Not an ignorant mob, by any means. Most of these men – and women too – could tell you something of the history of industry and the economic causes that had made the present cruelly competitive condition of society. ...Moreover, some of them were keen nature students; they could name the trees and wild flowers; give chapters for the wondrous tale of geology bearing on their local surroundings; whilst others had a considerable knowledge of the poets and literature. No, not an ignorant mob, but a crowd of people that had begun to think, and found out that the world was made not for the selfish and evil aggrandisement of a few, but for the fellowship and enjoyment of all."[159]

In the novel, as in real life, many of the participants arrived by bike. The Clarion Cycling Club struck deep roots across Lancashire and had several sections in East Lancashire, including Burnley, Accrington, Nelson and Barnoldswick. As well as the branches, there were a number of 'club houses' across the North in the late 1890s and early 1900s up to the start of the First World War. Amazingly, one survives, near Roughlee on the slopes of Pendle.

Taking tea at 'The Clarion'

Clarion ILP Tea Rooms, to use its full title, wasn't actually part of the 'Clarion' network of club houses but was owned separately, by Nelson Independent Labour Party (ILP). It was built in 1912, replacing a smaller club house nearby. For over a century 'The Clarion Tea Rooms' has been loved by walkers, cyclists and generations of socialists. It was visited by Keir Hardie and leading figures of the labour movement. But it isn't a sectarian hidey-hole. A couple of years ago they welcomed Michael Portillo and engaged in some gradely Lancashire banter with him.

Today it is run by the Nelson ILP Land Society and is one of the last remnants of that remarkably vital and inclusive socialist culture of East Lancashire that Clarke described in *The Red Flag*. And there's still an East Lancashire Clarion Choir which regularly performs at the tea rooms as well as other events across the North - West.[160]

---

[159] *The Red Flag* pp.163-4

[160] See the excellent history – *The Last Clarion House* (Ali Ronan) and its companion (published together) *ILP Clarion House – a Monument to a Movement* by Stan Iveson and Roger Brown, Nelson 2018

A couple of cycling veterans at Clarion House, Roughlee

The tea rooms, open ever Sunday throughout the year, are kept going by a team of volunteers. To sit on a bench or just luxuriate on the grass on a fine summer's day, with Pendle Hill above, chatting to other visitors or listening to the choir, is one of life's very special experiences.

22. Chartists, Owenites and Weavers

"Most interesting characters these old weavers of the first half of the last century – sturdy, thoughtful, independent, pioneering men, serious of soul yet sunny with the irrepressible Lancashire humour that will have its bit of cheery fun even in the darkest days..." [161]

Clarke was fascinated by the early history of the working class movement in Lancashire. At the heart of the radical movements that swept industrialising Lancashire in the early 1800s were the handloom weavers. In *Moorlands and Memories* he frequently refers to the little book called *Summer Evenings with Old Weavers*, written by the socialist and spiritualist James Swinglehurst in the 1880s. It describes chats in 'Bobby Heywood's Park', off Lever Street, with a group of elderly men who were active in the radical movements of the 1830s and 1840s.They had all been handloom weavers and they told the young author about their struggles for a better life – the ideals that later inspired the men and women whom Clarke describes in *The Red Flag*. Some were Owenites, others had been involved in the Chartist movement – or both.

The Luddites and Peterloo

Bolton was a hotbed of radical politics in the first half of the 19th century, well described in E.P. Thompson's magnificent book *The Making of the English Working Class*. As well as the early socialist ideas of Robert Owen – soon to inspire the Co-operative Movement – it was also a centre of underground, illegal activities in the movement known as 'Luddism'.

In 1812, many of the starving weavers from Bolton, Westhoughton and surrounding villages, staged an audacious assault on one of the new power-loom factories in Westhoughton. The attack was repulsed and many arrests were made. Several of the attackers – including a young boy of twelve – were executed in a shocking display of callousness.[162]

A few years later, on August 16th 1819, many working men and women from the Bolton area were attacked by the yeomanry on St Peter's Fields. Clarke refers to one of them in *Moorlands and Memories*, known as 'John o'Bolton, a handloom weaver who lived at Ainsworth. He attended the great demonstration and witnessed the massacre of defenceless men and women:

---

[161] *Moorlands* p.308

[162] See Bob Davies *The Luddites of Westhoughton*, 1972. J.T. Staton wrote a semi-fictional account of the episode in 'Luddites un Blackfaces', serialised in his *Bowtun Luminary* during 1853

..."*when he came home he had a sad and startling tale to tell his neighbours, eager to learn what had been going on in Manchester. He was emphatic they were wanton butchers. Later on, very naturally, when the Chartist movement started he joined it.*" [163]

Clarke recalls the story told to him by John o'Bolton's grand-daughter. He fell on hard times and the bailiffs came to his house, taking all they could lay their hands on – including even the Family Bible.

The violence of the Luddites was born out of sheer desperation. In Lancashire, in the years between 1810 and 1830, families were starving as the once-prosperous handloom weavers descended into poverty and hunger. Clarke was born in 1863, when only a few of the old weavers remained, with a handful carrying on their craft, weaving fancy quilts for a specialised market (see Chapter 12). By then, most weavers were young women working power-looms in huge sheds alongside Bolton's great spinning mil

A typical weaving shed in the 1900s, with row after row of Lancashire Looms. Weavers would typically manage four looms but in the early 20th century strikes broke out over attempts to get weavers to operate six or more looms

Another significant event in the pre-Chartist period was 'The Chatterton Fight', near Stubbins, on April 26th 1826. Surprisingly, Allen Clarke doesn't mention the pitched battle between soldiers and starving weavers, which led to the deaths of six people. There would have been many more but some of the soldiers were

---

[163] *Moorlands* p.281

sympathetic to the crowd and only struck them with the flats of their swords. A plaque in the village commemorates the tragic events.

The Lancashire Chartists

Clarke had a romantic fascination with the Chartists who rallied to the cause of 'the six points' for democratic reform, between 1837 and the late 1840s.[164] Bolton was a major centre of Chartist activity and in 1839 there was an armed attack on Little Bolton Town Hall. Whilst Clarke makes no mention of the 'Bolton Insurrection' he does wax lyrical about the huge gathering on Blackstone Edge in 1846 addressed by Ernest Jones, one of the most well-known of the Chartist leaders. Clarke writes:

"...in the days of Chartist agitation, that noble lover of humanity, Ernest Jones, addressed a great gathering of working folks (August, 1846). He wrote a poem about Blackstone Edge:

> *Waved the wind on Blackstone height*
> *A standard of the broad sunlight,*
> *And sung that morn with trumpet might,*
> *A sounding song for liberty*!"[165]

Many of those gathered on Blackstone Edge would have been from nearby Rochdale, whose leader was Tom Livsey. His political career encompassed Co-operation, Chartism and ultimately Liberalism. Clarke's Rochdale-based novel of Co-operation and Chartism, *The Men Who Fought for Us*, features Livsey extensively. Clarke introduces him to the reader as the Chartist General Strike of 1842 (see below) is gathering strength.

Lancashire and Yorkshire unites under the red flag! A May Day meet-up on Blackstone Edge. The great gathering of 1846 has been revived and in 'normal times' crowds make their way up to the 'tops' to celebrate our radical Chartist heritage

---

[164] The six points were based on demands for universal make suffrage, though some Chartists supported demands for women's enfranchisement as well. See Malcolm Chase *Chartism: a new history*, 2007

[165] *Moorlands* p.287

In the chapter 'At The Chartist and Socialist Meeting' Livsey argues with those who want to escalate the strike, pointing out the heavy military presence in the town: *"They'd rejoice if we'd only no more gumption than kick up a bit of a bother, an' give 'em the opportunity they're waiting for. We're hurtin' 'em far more by doin' nowt than doin' summat just now. "*[166]

An early biography of Livsey was written by Margaret Rebecca Lahee, better known as a dialect poet who is one of the four poets commemorated on The Lancashire Dialect Writers' Memorial in Rochdale.[167]

Clarke mentions the old inn at Five Houses on Winter Hill, where he suggests Chartists used to meet in secret; it was sufficiently remote to escape the notice of the authorities. [168]He is romancing slightly. Chartists were able to meet publicly by then (the 1840s) though there's no doubt that many of the weavers and miners who did gather at Five Houses would have supported the Chartist cause. But it's a good story, and perhaps some of the earlier radicals, such as the Luddites who were very much a 'secret society', may have met at the lonely beer-house on the moors to plan insurrection over a glass of 'whoam-brewed'. My kind of revolution.

The Plug and Sherry Riots of 1842

The local history of the Chartist movement remains relatively unexplored. And it is at the very local level that Chartism is so fascinating as a political and social movement. It tended to ebb and flow with great surges of activity followed by relative decline. In 1842 one of the most well-known events was 'the Chartist General Strike', also known as 'The Plug Plot Riots'. The 'plugs' in question were the fusible boiler plugs in the boilers which kept the mills going. Remove them, and the mill stopped. During August 1842, groups of what we might call today 'flying pickets' went from town to town removing the boiler plugs and urging their fellow workers to make common cause with them. It was not, however, just another 'wages' dispute. It was an all-out insurrection to get working class political power, through the vote. The flying pickets had brought out the mills of Bury, then turned their attention to the textile factories of Bolton, heading along Bury New Road:

"Desperate in distress, on an August day in 1842, a large mob marched from Bury along this road over the moor, making for Bolton. They took the plugs out of factory boilers on the way. They were joined by other contingents from the

---

[166] *The Men Who Fought For Us* p.63

[167] Lahee was born in Ireland and became an important part of Rochdale's literary community

[168] *Moorlands* p.120

surrounding districts and from Bolton. When they neared Bolton they were met by the Yeomanry Cavalry – there was a scuffle and many injured, but no fatalities, a considerable number of the rioters being taken to prison."[169]

Many of the crowd headed back towards Bury and besieged the home of a local doctor in Ainsworth, demanding food and drink. Perhaps the emphasis was more on drink. Whatever, the diplomatic medic explained that he had only a small amount of sherry in the house so he diluted it with ten parts water, offering a drink to all who wanted one. The throng continued on their way home, evidently satisfied.[170]

Clarke frequently refers to an old Chartist character known as 'Radical Grimshaw'. He appears in *Moorlands and Memories* and also in some of Clarke's novels:

"*Somewhere between Christ's Church and Crook's factory, in one of the wayside cottages, dwelt an old man you could not help noticing, a conspicuous figure with a white tall hat. My father said he was an old Chartist, and was known as Radical Grimshaw*." He adds that his friend John Kirkman wrote to him with news of the old man's death, lamenting that "*like most reformers of his class, he died in the workhouse*." [171]

The first literary description of Grimshaw is in Clarke's early novel *The Knobstck*, where he appears as 'Joe Carklan', an Irish name. A more obvious reference is in *The Cotton Panic*, set during the Lancashire Cotton Famine between 1861 and 1864, where Clarke introduces an old handloom-weaver known as 'Chartist Grimshaw'.

The second half of the 19th century was less tumultuous in Lancashire politics. Trade unionism emerged as a powerful force amongst the skilled, mostly male, textile workers. The 'operative mule spinners' were amongst the most well-organised group of workers in the country and developed a sophisticated system of industrial relations with the employers. Clarke's father was a union delegate for the spinners' union though he found to his cost that there were limits to employer paternalism. When Clarke was a young boy his father was blacklisted for his union activities.

The Great Strike of 1887

The most sensational industrial dispute in Bolton in the second half of the century

---

[169] *Moorlands* p.283

[170] I am grateful to Ainsworth Local History Society for this story

[171] *Moorlands* pp.17-8

was 'The Great Engineers' Strike' of 1887. It had a big impact on Clarke and many other young workers who were drawn into the embryonic socialist party, the Social Democratic Federation. Writing of the heavily industrialised Higher Bridge Street area, he says:

"In Jubilee Year, 1887, this Higher Bridge Street and neighbourhood saw exciting doings in connection with the engineers' strike, when hundreds of special constables and military (camped on Spa Road Recreation Ground) were brought into the town, an there were disturbances and riots around Dobson's foundry where many 'knobsticks' conveyed to the works from the station, were working. On the 1st of July the soldiers charged the mob, and several persons were severely injured. More than once I saw the angry crowds gather round the vehicles containing the blacklegs. The strike lasted six months."[172]

The strike inspired Clarke's second novel, *The Knobstick* (an old Lancashire term for blackleg). It was serialised in *The Trotter* and then published in book form in 1893. The novel has some memorable scenes of the strike as well as some touching stories about working class solidarity and compassion. It was acclaimed by the East German literary critic Mary Ashraf as the outstanding 'novel of textile workers and engineers'. [173]

The story of the 1887 strike was researched by Bill Dagnall, the district secretary of the Engineers' Union in the 1970s. Sadly it has never been published but it would be a worthwhile project. Bill was, in many ways, a modern equivalent of 'Radical Grimshaw' – a self-educated working class intellectual who was a delight to talk with.

The Dobbill Do

The story of industrial relations in the textile industry was generally one of orderly negotiations and compromise, though occasionally things could turn nasty. This happened 'up Daubhill' in 1906 when the large employers Tootal and Broadhurst attempted to introduce new technology in their huge Sunnyside Mills weaving sheds. Instead of the standard four looms worked by one weaver, new 'patent automatic looms', could operate with one weaver managing six looms. Whilst this resulted in a significant 'speeding up' of the process, the employers were not prepared to offer an increase in pay rates. The strike was long and bitter, mostly involving women weavers, who by then were highly unionised. Clarke publicised

---

[172] *Moorlands* p.189

[173] Mary Ashraf *The Novel of Textile Workers and Engineers*, Halle University 1976. Also see *An Introduction to English Working Class Literature*, Berlin 1982, which discusses the work of Clarke and his friend James Haslam

the strike and the weavers cause in his *Northern Weekly* and featured a weekly letter, in dialect, from 'Billy Pickinpeg' about the goings on, referred to as 'The Dobbill Do'. 'Billy' may have been Clarke himself; the letters are funny and ironic, making fools of the employers, 'knobsticks' and police, satirising the 'patent automatic cemetery looms'.

Sunnyside Mills were demolished in the early 1970s. A feature of the mills was the stone friezes, expertly-wrought sculpture depicting the cotton manufacturing process. Fortunately most of them were saved and now adorn the Market Place shopping centre on Bridge Street (see Chapter 5).

Whilst Sunnyside Mill is only a memory, the enormous Swan Lane Mills - once the biggest spinning mills in the world - have survived in multiple occupancy. I hope they will not fall victim to demolition like Sunnyside or more recently the destruction of the graceful Beehive Mills in Great Lever, where my mum once worked on 'the housewives' shift in the evenings.

Daubhill itself is every bit as lively and diverse now as it was in Clarke's time, when he describes it as a thriving working class area with a large Irish community. He knew it well, having been born at the bottom end of Derby Street and attended local schools. Clarke himself represented the mix of cultures in Victorian Bolton, having an Irish father and an English mother.

23. A Guid Doctor – Dr John Johnston MD

Hurrah for the Cycle, swift, trusty and strong!
May it daily win loves and stay with us long!
Good luck let is wish to the Courser of steel,
And Health and Long Life to the Men of the Wheel! [174]

Dr John Johnston, the co-founder of the Bolton Whitman group whom we met earlier, was a friend of Clarke's. He pops up in *Moorlands and Memories* on a couple of occasions, in different contexts. He was a man who wore many hats – that of doctor, poet, cyclist, traveller, photographer and more. Clarke describes him as *"one of our local bards and a great bicycle traveller who has issued many books and pamphlets."*[175]

Johnston was a proud Scot, born in Annan, Dumfriesshire, in 1852. He moved to Bolton in 1876 as a GP, after having qualified as doctor at Edinburgh in 1874 followed by a two year stint as hospital surgeon at West Bromwich. He lived initially at 2 Bridgeman Street before moving to 54 Manchester Road. He always kept his Annan links and the best source of reports on his Whitmanite activities is in the columns of *The Annandale Observer*.[176] Clarke shared the doctor's love of Whitman's poetry and the two men cycled together on occasions.

Dr John Johnston MD

Visiting Walt

Johnston visited Walt Whitman in New Jersey in 1890, to be followed by Wallace the following year. His impressions, including his professional-standard photographs, were published by the Manchester Labour Press. After

---

[174] John Johnston, *Musa Medica*, 1897 p.133

[175] *Moorlands* p. 300

[176] *The Annandale Observer* carried an article on his appointment to the post of Medical Superintendent at Townley's. October 26th 1917

Wallace's visit the following year a 'combined volume' of the two men's impressions of their hero was published by Allen and Unwin. [177]

Johnston's description of his meeting with Whitman, hours after he had disembarked after his trans-Atlantic crossing, is anything but under-stated:

"The first thing about himself that struck me was the physical immensity and magnificent proportions of the man, and next, the picturesque majesty of his presence as a whole..." He goes on to write of Whitman's "irresistible magnetism of his sweet, aromatic presence, which seemed to exhale sanity, purity, and naturalness, and exercised over me an attraction which positively astonished me, producing an exaltation of mind and soul which no man's presence ever did before. I felt that I was here face to face with the living embodiment of all that was good, noble and lovable in humanity."[178]

The conversation with Whitman was recorded as precisely as possible, though Johnston states *"He talked so freely, and so unconstrainedly, that I cannot possibly note down all that he said, and the following are mere scraps of his most interesting talk : 'That must be a very nice little circle of friends you have at Bolton.' I assented, and he went on – 'I hope you will tell them how deeply sensible I am of their appreciation and regard for me....'"*[179]

The meeting went well; Whitman invited him round again the following day. They met and went down to Camden Wharf with his carer, Warren Fritzinger, who was in charge of Whitman's wheelchair. There is a fine photograph of the two at Camden Wharf, taken by Johnston. They had two more meetings and Whitman gave him a framed portrait of himself to present to Wallace.

A photo of Whitman with his carer Warren Fritzinger at Camden Wharf, taken by Johnston during his 1890 trip

[177] John Johnston MD *A Visit to Walt Whitman and some of his friends in 1890*, Manchester Labour Press 1890; J. Johnston MD and J.W. Wallace *Visits to Walt Whitman 1890-1891* London, 1917

[178] *A Visit to Walt Whitman* pp.23-6

[179] *A Visit to Walt Whitman* pp.32-3

As Johnston departs, he is told: *"Good-bye, Doctor, good-bye! Give my love to Wallace and the rest of the fellows, and tell them that I hope they won't over-estimate Walt Whitman. He doesn't set up to be a finished anything.."* [180]

Johnston spent the rest of his time in America visiting friends of Whitman's including Andrew Rome in Brooklyn (who had Annan connections) and naturalist John Burroughs, further out of the city up the Hudson Valley. He also met Whitman's close friend Herbert Gilchrist.

Nearly a hundred years later I travelled in Johnston's footsteps. I met relatives of John Burroughs in 'upstate' New York and Whitman scholars including Ed Folsom in Iowa, Gay Wilson Allen in New Jersey, Charles Feinberg in Detroit, and Joanne Krieg in New York City, amongst many more. Charles, Gay and Joanne have all passed on but contact between Bolton and the American 'Whitmanites', including Ed Folsom, Karen Karbiener, Mike Robertson and others have continued and grown.

The medical man

Johnston was a highly skilled physician, trained at Edinburgh where he gained his MD. As well as his 'day job' as a GP he found time to be an instructor for the Lancashire and Yorkshire Railway's ambulance classes. This brought him into direct contact with the realities of daily life on Britain's railways, and the dangers faced by railwaymen. In his diary for 1887 he records the death of a shunter at Trinity Street station, Mr William Davies. He fell off a truck and was run over – both his legs were broken and his left foot was cut off. He died from his injuries: *"The poor fellow was one of the members of my ambulance class and has left a wife and five children. Alas! Alas!"*

In addition to his work as an instructor for both the railway ambulance classes he acted as a judge at many railway ambulance competitions, including those of the London and North Western Railway and Great Central Railway. These contests were major events which continued well into the 1960s but have sadly died out.

During the First World War he served at the vast Whalley Military Hospital before moving on to Townley's Hospital where he was appointed Medical Superintendent in September 1917. In *Moorlands and Memories* Clarke writes of Townley's Hospital during the First World War, still a very recent memory, and how *"many boys in the characteristic blue suit of the wounded and invalid soldier have sat on the seats at the Great Lever tram terminus, close to Townley's Hospital."*[181]

---

[180] *A Visit to Walt Whitman* p.85

[181] *Moorlands* p.299

In Johnston's diary there is a particularly moving entry where he describes a soldier pleading with him to amputate his hand so that he wouldn't have to return to his regiment. Johnston records: that *"We decided that to attempt its removal might involve some risk to the future usefulness of his hand and we therefore counselled it being left alone. 'Danger or no danger' said the soldier to me, 'I want you to do the operation, I'd rather lose my hand than go back yonder'. He meant The Front – 'it's Hell!'*[182]

Johnston and his Whitmanite friends, with the doctor looking more self-conscious than usual in full military uniform. L-R: Broadhurst, Thompson, Johnston, Wild, Wallace, Wentworth Dixon, Minnie Whiteside, Nightingale. Taken c 1916

Little wonder that Johnston's experience of the War turned him into a pacifist, even though he seems to have liked the trappings of his military uniform, in which he was sometimes photographed, at Whitman gatherings during the war. We are all masses of contradictions.

The Workhouse

Townley's Hospital was built next to The Fishpools Institution – the workhouse, a name to strike fear into working class people in Bolton. Clarke wrote of *"that*

[182] Diaries of Dr John Johnston, Bolton Library

place we all desire to avoid, that place which has always been such a terror to the poor."

However, the route to the workhouse was not without its charms; it can still be walked or cycled today. The original track ran from Rishton Lane, along the 'ginnel' by the railway 'bordered with upright sleepers' as he described. They were still there in the 1960s but have gone now. The ginnel was known as 'Lovers' Walk'. Clarke recalls:

"Sometimes I have seen workhouse inmates on this path, returning to the place after an afternoon out, pass lovers loitering along oblivious of everything but their paradise, perhaps never thinking that once upon a time some of these old pauper men and women were young and in love like them."[183]

I remember the path very well, though I never heard it called 'Lovers' Walk'. By the early 1960s the line was derelict though there were some remains of the old Plodder Lane locomotive shed, which was adjacent to the hospital. When I was incarcerated at Townley's with 'yellow jaundice' at the age of about seven one of the compensations was watching the occasional freight train going past the ward window.

Like most Boltonians, I was born at Townley's and perhaps the sound and smell of steam locomotives at a very early age gave me my love of railways. I used to play with my mates on the path and sometimes we would creep round the ruin of the former Nurses' Home on the opposite side of the railway, convincing ourselves it was haunted. The ginnel still follows its original course, winding round what used to be the loco sheds on an 'S' bend, before getting to Plodder Lane, where the original station was located.

There's a story about a group of young engine cleaners at Plodder Lane loco shed fooling the signalman at Plodder Lane by 'ringing off shed' and pretending to be a locomotive. It was a dark evening and the group of lads walked past the signalbox carrying a couple of 'white' head- lamps as the front of an engine and a red tail lamp at the rear. The signalman was convinced it was a loco going down to Great Moor Street station – but it never arrived at the next signalbox, Lever Street. A search party was sent out to find the 'missing engine' but, unsurprisingly, there was no sign of engine or lamps. A good example of Bolton trotting.

Today, the path forms part of a national cycleway Route 55 and is well used. But I wish the railway had survived. My grandad ('Tom') was the last regular user of Plodder Lane station, travelling to Monton Green each day to his job at the

---

[183] *Moorlands* p.300

Nasmyth engineering factory in Patricroft.

Johnston and Clarke would have been great champions of cycle networks. A hundred years ago there wasn't really much need for segregated cycle routes as motorised traffic was very limited. One of the few positive outcomes of the current 'Pandemic' is that people have got their old bikes out, given them a rub-down and a bit of oil, and rediscovered the pleasures of cycling on quiet roads. I hope it lasts, but there's no doubt we will need our 'off road' routes, and many more of them.

As well as a practical way of getting around, Johnston had a modern view of healthiness and well-being. Clarke quotes from his poem 'Doctor Air':

"There's Dr Blister, Dr Bleed, and old-fashioned Dr Pill,

Who with mixtures, potions, draughts, will cure your every ill;

And Dr Sanitation will with wonder make you stare,

But the king of all the doctors, new or old, is Doctor Air" [184]

The move to Lostock

Johnston and his wife Bertha moved to a more salubrious part of Bolton that was convenient for his other preferred form of transport – the train. From the early 1900s he gives his address as 'Sunny Brae', Lostock Junction Lane. The fine Edwardian house still stands. I wonder if the present occupants know that their home hosted many of the Whitamanite garden parties, where excerpts from *Leaves of Grass* were read, the 'loving cup' with spiced claret being passed around, followed by speeches from 'the master' Wallace and often Johnston himself. [185]

A civic activist

The name of Dr Johnston crops up in many accounts of 'civic' activities in Bolton between the 1880s and First World War. Like Wallace he was active in the early Independent Labour Party and Labour Church but also played high-profile roles in a range of local institutions, including Bolton Lads' Club, civic societies and numerous medical associations.

---

[184] *Moorlands* p. 301 and in John Johnston *Musa Medica* p.26

[185] See Paul Salveson *With Walt Whitman in Bolton*; p.20 gives an example of the garden party at Fred Wild's. Johnston is down on the invitation to give a talk on 'The Evolution of Life and Consciousness'

He chaired a meeting of Bolton's Progressive League and Housing and Town Planning Society at New Spinners' Hall in October 1912 when Edward Carpenter spoke on 'Beauty in Civic Life'. There was a strong lobby in Bolton and elsewhere to 'beautify' industrial towns (Oldham had its 'Beautiful Oldham Society' led by Mary Higgs). Johnston was active in Bolton's Housing and Town Planning Society which hosted the lectures by T.H. Mawson on 'Bolton as it is and as it might be'.[186]

He was strongly opposed to child labour, sharing Clarke's outrage at the half-time system still extensively operated in the Bolton mills at the turn of the century. His book *Wastage of Child Life* (1909) was a denunciation of child labour, using his home town as an example, the book being sub-titled *as exemplified by conditions in Lancashire*.[187]

The—
PROGRESSIVE LEAGUE,
and the Bolton Housing and Town Planning Association.

Monday Evening, October 21st
At 7-30 in the
NEW SPINNERS' HALL,
St. George's Road,

A LECTURE
BY
Edward Carpenter, M.A.
Author of "Towards Democracy."
SUBJECT:
"BEAUTY IN CIVIC LIFE."

Dr. J. JOHNSTON, of Lostock, will Preside.

Admission Free. Retiring Collection.
Tickets for Reserved Seats, One Shilling each.
From Mr. W. M. Farrington, or Mr. J. Darbyshire, 7 Corporation Chambers, Corporation Street, or at the door.

GEO. S. IKIN, Typ., Fold St., Bolton.

A poster advertising a meeting of the Progressive League, October 21st 1912. Edward Carpenter is speaking on 'Beauty in Civic Life' with Johnston presiding

He was a man of advanced 'liberal' views and became a close friend of the gay socialist Edward Carpenter, becoming his (unpaid) physician. The two, with Carpenter's lover George Merrill, went on holiday together to Morocco. Johnston and Wallace were particularly close friends, even to the extent of sharing each others' beds on occasions. [188]

He had a long marriage to Bertha and they shared several cycling holidays in Britain and abroad. They moved to Bispham in the early 1920s when he became ill. He died in September 1927, outliving Wallace by a year though his final years were blighted by poor health.

---

[186] T.H. Mawson *Bolton as it is and as it might be – six lectures delivered under the auspices of the Bolton Housing and Town Planning Society*, Bolton and London, 1916
[187] John Johnston *Wastage of Child Life*, Manchester 1908 and reprinted by The Fabian Society 1909
[188] William Broadhurst *An Address in Memory of the Late J.W. Wallace, Wentworth Dixon Dr J. Johnston,* December 6th 1930, Bolton. He talked of Johnston's "love of Wallace and his reverence for him". The reference to them sharing a bed together is in Michael Robertson's *Worshipping Walt – Whitman's Disciples*, 2008. pp.214-6

24. Rambling about: groups and gatherings

"So long as there are ramble clubs there is hope for the world" - Allen Clarke

"This rambling is excellent for health. It blesses the body, feeds the mind, promotes good fellowship. Riches may be alright – I don't know, never having had any...but I do know that Dame Nature and a jolly rambling company bring us about as near heaven as anybody may expect on earth."[189]

Clarke was a very sociable man and loved developing 'networks' – with himself usually at the centre, it has to be said. On one level this was very clever promotion for his publications, creating what some now call 'relationship marketing'. The picnics, gatherings, tea parties as well as the rambling and cycling clubs, helped to re-inforce a loyal readership. But it would be unfair to suggest it was purely a cynical way of boosting his market. He genuinely enjoyed the conviviality and did much to encourage new writers.

By the 1890s rambling and cycling had become popular working class activities. However poor you were, to go for a walk on the nearby moors all you needed was a good pair of boots. Rambling groups flourished in the Lancashire towns, linked to churches, the socialist movement (not least 'The Clarion') and other institutions.

In *Moorlands and Memories* Clarke refers to the activities of the Blackburn Ramble Club. In 1905 they produced a very attractive bound volume of walks around Lancashire, with a sequel the following year. *The Rambler* described itself as 'a record of rambles, historical facts, legends and nature notes' and was edited by J.T. Fielding. It's a lovely book, one of my most precious.[190]

The Labour Church and James Sims

Moorlands and Memories is full of references to rambling and cycling groups, particularly The Bolton 'Sunday Afternoon Class' organised by the Labour Church; it was one of the earlier rambling groups which had a broad appeal. As we've seen, the 'Labour Church' was a socialist-leaning group that wasn't tied to any political body, though it was close to the Independent Labour Party. It wasn't a theological movement in the conventional sense, but aped the forms of religion through hymns and its' ethical approach. It was very much a Northern phenomenon, with most of its branches in Lancashire and the West Riding. [191]

---

[189] *Teddy Ashton's Lancashire Annual* 1921

[190] *The Rambler*, vol. 1, Darwen 1905. Volume 2, equally impressive, was published the following year

[191] See my forthcoming *Walt Whitman and the Religion of Socialism*

A sylvan scene in Yarnsdale Quarry with the Blackburn Ramblers, c 1905. Unlike the ILP and Clarion walking and cycling groups, at this time the Blackburn Rambling Club seems to have been predominantly male

Bolton had a particularly active group between its formation in 1892 and the First World War, and included Wallace and Johnston and other members of the Whitman circle, Clarke himself and Alice Collinge who was the organist. It was led by the venerable figure of James Sims, who lived on Church Bank, close to the parish church.[192] Sims was a botanist and led many of the walks that Clarke describes, together with John Fletcher of Westhoughton, a coal miner. The programme of walks began in the Spring and finished in late Autumn, after which the group met indoors until better weather returned. From 1900 they used the Central Hall at Acresfield for the 'indoors' season. Clarke often joined the walks:

"I have recollections of enjoyable and instructive rambles over Winter Hill with the Bolton Sunday Afternoon Class (in connection with the Labour Church) led by that sturdy reformer and rambler, John Kirkman, and by that clever collier-botanist of Westhoughton, and gipsy teas, made by a spirit-kettle, on the moors."[193]

James Sims eventually moved to the Fylde, living a small cottage where he pursued his interest in mosses. Clarke describes, in *Windmill Land*, meeting him and walking to Little Marton Mill:

---

[192] There is a fascinating interview in *Northern Weekly* with Sims, by 'Leon Gray' (possible James Haslam) where Sims outlines his own beliefs and the activities of the Labour Church in Bolton. May 11th 1901

[193] *Moorlands* pp.120-1

"He was an old Chartist – from Bolton ....a reformer, an agitator – and a good botanist, as so many of the old weavers were, his speciality being mosses....He showed me the mosses, with their silver stalks and scarlet and golden caps, just like the fairies of our nursery takes, in hedge-side and on garden wall; and it was a revelation of the infinite beauty that God packs into small things."[194]

The Clarion networks

At much the same time as the Labour Church was at its height, the Clarion Cycling Club, and rambling and naturalists' sections, were gaining popularity.

Many 'Labour Church-ers' would have been involved in the Clarion movement, reading Robert Blatchford's popular socialist paper, initially published in Manchester. Very much like the Labour Church's 'Sunday Afternoon Class', *The Clarion* newspaper and its off-shoots encouraged interest in the world about us. It had groups of field naturalists dotted around the North and the newspaper carried regular articles by Harry Lowerison, the 'Field Clubs' co-ordinator, on wild flowers and trees. [195]

In *Moorlands and Memories* Clarke mentions the cycling club several times, including the helpful sign erected at the bottom of the hill approaching Whalley, cautioning cyclists to 'slow down' before the tight bend over the Ribble bridge.

The Ribble Valley Clarion Club House at Ribchester, c1900

---

[194] *Windmill Land,* 1916 p.56

[195] Several were published in *Sweet Briar Sprays,* sub-titled 'being posies pluckt in a random walk through this still beautiful England of ours', 1899

For many years, Clarke was a close friend of Blatchford and his editorial team and occasionally attended the annual 'meets'. The Clarion Cycling Club reached its high-point in terms of membership just before the Second World War. In the 1950s and 60s the combination of changing lifestyles, car ownership and the decline of that 'ethical socialist' culture which 'The Clarion' movement was so much a part of, led to its virtual disappearance. Yet as we've seen the Clarion tea rooms at Pendle have survived, as well as some branches of the cycling club. Some, for example Brighton Clarion, remain faithful to the club's socialist traditions, though others abjure 'politics'.

In 1982 a few of us in Bolton decided to re-form a Bolton section, only to find it was still – just about – alive, with four elderly members including Sid Clemmett and 'Young' Tommy Higham, still getting out on their bikes, well into their 70s.[196]

The *Northern Weekly* fellowships and after

Clarke edited *Teddy Ashton's Northern Weekly* from 1896 to 1908, though it went through several changes of name. From around 1900 he started to promote *Northern Weekly* groups, notably cycling and walking. There were local branches, usually managed by members of Clarke's network. Most of the walks were local, sometimes involving short train journeys.

It was after the war, and following the end of Clarke's own editorial responsibilities, that he devoted more time to group activities from his base in Blackpool. Using his weekly column in *The Liverpool Weekly Post* he promoted a regular programme of walks and cycle rides.

The post-war rambling boom and the Blackpool clubs

The First World War was a surprisingly productive time for Clarke, writing regular features in *The Bolton Journal and Guardian, Liverpool Weekly Post* and other papers. But the opportunity for group rides was limited – most of the male riders were at the front and some were in prison as conscientious objectors. When peace returned, the number of walking groups started to grow:

"One is pleased to find Ramble Clubs increasing. Beside the Naturalists' Society, there are several in Bolton, one at least in connection with a place of worship, Albert Place United Methodist Ramble Club which meets every Saturday afternoon."[197] He mentions that the club is *"open to both ladies and gentlemen, as*

---

[196] See Denis Pye *Fellowship is Life: The National Clarion Cycling Club 1895 - 1995*, Bolton 1995

[197] *Moorlands* p.339

all Ramble Clubs ought to be."

However, it was in Blackpool where Clarke developed his most successful network of walking and cycling clubs. The Blackpool Ramble Club was formed in 1920 and grew to a membership of several hundred. A feature of the Club's activities was welcoming holiday-makers to Blackpool on their walks. Alongside the ramble club was the 'Speedwell Cycling Fellowship'. In his *Lancashire Annual* for 1921, he writes:

"This year (1920) in various Lancashire towns and districts have been started 'Speedwell' clubs for outdoor recreation and good fellowship." He goes on to point out that the membership fee is 2/6 which includes a badge – *"an enamel blue flower with white centre – the Speedwell flower that you find along the waysides in June"*. [198]

The secretary was a 'J. Clarke' of 94 Mornington Road, Bolton. This is almost certainly his brother Joe, who is pictured alongside Allen Clarke at 'Teddy Ashton's Well'. Clarke's last Bolton address was 104 Mornington Road so they would have been close neighbours.

He promoted the various 'Speedwell' groups through *The Liverpool Weekly Post* for which, by the 1920s, he had a regular column. Blackpool activities were publicised in the local *Gazette and Herald*. The Blackpool club emerged as the largest, often attracting two hundred walkers. I remember an old Blackpudlian talking about one of the walks which involved getting the train from Blackpool Central station. The crowd sang one of Clarke's 'ramble songs' to the entertainment of the driver and fireman, who joined in with gusto!

During 1921 a number of 'Speedwell' meetings were organised, sometimes involving both walking and cycling groups. *The Lancashire Annual* has a charming photo (see above) of 'Speedwell Cyclists and Ramblers' outside the People's Hall, Chester, on August Bank Holiday Sunday. The group is quite mixed with several children as well as men and women. There were other 'general meets' during the year at Barrow Bridge and Blackpool.[199]

---

[198] 'Speedwell Rambling and Cycling Clubs' *Teddy Ashton's Lancashire Annual* December 1921, p.105
[199] *Lancashire Annual* 1921, p.106

Photo. by Hughes, Wigan.

Speedwell Cyclists and Ramblers at Chester, August Bank Holiday Sunday, 1921.

An intriguing photo from *Lancashire Annual* of a group of Speedwell Ramblers and Cyclists at 'The People's Hall', most likely in Chester, August Bank Holiday 1921

25. Over Holcombe Hill and Fo'Edge

"I have many picnic memories of Holcombe Hill – of a 'Teddy Ashton' gathering there, and the woman who brought the 'fatty cakes'."[200]

Clarke often cycled over the moorland road out of Bolton past what used to be 'The Lamb' pub and on through Hawkshaw village to Ramsbottom. Holcombe Hill was one of his favourite meeting haunts for his *Northern Weekly* group of writers. I never found out who the woman was who brought the 'fatty cakes'.

On Holcombe Hill – one of the helpful Peak and Northern signs to help walkers find their way

It remains a beautiful place to walk and admire the moorland scenery stretching across towards Rochdale and Knowl Hill. If you stand on the top of Holcombe Hill and look across to the east you will see, if you look carefully, Cowpe reservoir. Above it is Fo' Edge and perhaps the most important – certainly the loveliest – shrine to a Lancashire writer. Let's explore the area.

A moorland grave and a village poet

Follow Clarke's cycle route from Bradshaw and you'll get to the former mill village of Hawkshaw, where another of Clarke's friends lived and wrote. John Fawcett Skelton was very much 'the village poet' and published a collection called *Hawkshaw Lane and Other Poems*.[201]

---

200 *Moorlands* p.261

201 John Fawcett Skelton *Hawkshaw Lane and Other Poems*, Bury n.d.

He penned a tribute to Roger Worthington, a local Baptist minister who died in 1709. His solitary grave still remains, next to Lower Grainings and near to Holcombe Hey Fold, where he lived. It's publicly accessible and worth a visit. There's even a bench and a picnic table to enjoy a Skelton wrote about the unkempt state the grave had fallen into:

> *"There just below Broadstone Delph*
> *In an unbounded cemetery to himself,*
> *Lies Roger Worthington, an old divine,*
> *Whose gravestone bears the date of seventeen-nine,*
> *A Baptist minister he, who bought the ground*
> *And left to somebody a yearly pound*
> *To keep his lonely tombstone nice and neat,*
> *But that somebody has proved a cheat,*
> *For now in moss-grown fragments, sad to see,*
> *Old Roger's tablet lies upon the lea."*[202]

The grave is just below Holcombe Hill. From here there are fine views across Bolton and over to Manchester. Reddisher (in the past, often spelt 'Radisher') Woods is a beautiful spot, very well landscaped with delightful paths and remains of old industry. You can walk up past Taylor's Farm and along Moorbottom Road, and curve round to the summit, Peel Tower. It was erected in 1846 to mark the abolition of the hated Corn Laws and to celebrate Peel's role in the campaign. Another way of reaching Roger's Grave is to walk from Edgworth by Red Earth Farm (an equestrian centre).

A good tip for a circular walk is to continue through Holcombe Hey Farm and pass 'Paddy's Pond' to your left. It probably fed a mill at the bottom of the clough; the pond was restored by the Ministry of Defence. 'Paddy' was Col. P. V. Panton OBE, who served as CO of the 1st Battalion The Queen's Regiment.

Drop down and cross the stream at 'Bottoms' (site of the old mill) and pass the remains of Holcombe Head Farm. You get on to Moorbottom Road – but it's really just a very rough track, taking you round in a horse-shoe and back towards Edgworth. It's quite spectacular.

A moorland murder

Today, Holcombe Hill is a popular area for walkers, with the summit offering magnificent views across to Bury, Salford and Manchester. Close to Holcombe Hill, heading past Pilgrim's Cross towards Helmshore, is the memorial to Ellen Strange,

---

[202] *Moorlands* p.261

A very special 'sacred place' – Roger Worthington's Grave above Hawkshaw

a woman who was murdered in the late 18th century. At first sight there seem to be similarities with the killing of Lizzie Holt in Longworth Clough, though it appears that the murderer was her husband. Various stories have been put forward about her tragic and brutal death. According to The Holcombe Village Society the facts only emerged quite recently:

"Research of old records suggested that Ellen Strange was murdered between midnight and one o'clock on January 26, 1761. Her death was

described in detail at an inquest two days later. She was however called Ellen Broadley and had been married to John Broadley, a labourer from Clayton-le-Moors, for some ten years but kept her maiden name, as was commonplace in East Lancashire at the time. The couple were paupers and travelled in search of work. There is also evidence that their relationship endured bouts of heavy drinking and violence. One theory is that they quarrelled the night before the murder and Ellen may have been trying to make her way to the Strange family home at Ash Farm, near Hawkshaw. Under a full moon, Broadley supposedly pursued and murdered her. He was tried at Lancaster Assizes but acquitted through lack of eye witnesses to the killing. The jury may have spared him from the gallows because he had reported finding Ellen's body... but was this a ploy to divert suspicion from himself? Broadley was freed and died seven years later." [203]

The Ellen Strange Cairn, annual gathering July 2020. *Photo courtesy Martin McMulkin*

There is an annual walk to the memorial, remembering all those who have died as a result of domestic violence. It's organised by The Endeavour Trust which supports the victims of domestic abuse.

Edwin Waugh and Waugh's Well

Let's lighten the tone a bit and have a look at Waugh's Well. It's one of the prettiest spots in Lancashire, celebrating the doyen of Lancashire poets.

But who was he? Edwin Waugh (1817-1890) - 'the Lancashire Burns' - spent most of his adult life in Rochdale, the Lancashire town that has probably produced more dialect writers per square mile than anywhere else in the county. It is right and fitting that Rochdale has its 'dialect writers' memorial' in Broadfield Park, which was erected in 1900. Waugh, naturally, features on it, along with Trafford Clegg, Margaret Lahee and Oliver Ormerod. Bolton should have its own! In fact, every

---

[203] Holcombe Village Society website and Helmshore Local History Society, in John Simpson *Ellen Strange, a Moorland Mystery Explained, 1989*

Lancashire town has a good crop of writers who should be celebrated. Waugh has done well, with the Rochdale memorial, Fo' Edge and also 'The Edwin Waugh' Wetherspoon's in Heywood. That particular bit of recognition is ironic given his long struggle with alcoholism. But I like the pub.

Waugh began 'the dialect boom' of the second half of the 19th century, largely through the success of his poem 'Come Whoam to Thi Childer An' Me', first published in 1856. It is the cry of a working class wife, pleading with her husband, to leave the pub and come back to the family home. Oh, go on then, here's a taster:

> *"Well aw've just mended th'fire wi' a cob;*
> *Owd Swaddle has brought thi new shoon;*
> *There's some nice bacon-collops o' th' hob,*
> *An' a quart o' ale-posset i' th' oon;*
> *Aw've brought thi top-cwot, doesta know,*
> *For th' rain's comin' deawn very dree;*
> *An' th' har-stone's as white as new snow;*
> *Come whoam to thi childer an' me.*
> *An' th' har-stone's as white as new snow;*
> *Come whoam to thi childer an' me."*[204]

As well as the slightly moralistic poems like 'Come Whoam', Waugh wrote of the high moorlands and the characters that inhabited them, in both dialect and standard English.

The Dialect Writers' Memorial (a rather forbidding monument it has to be said) isn't the only monument to Waugh. Perhaps a more fitting tribute is 'Waugh's Well', on Fo' Edge ('Fall Edge'), high above Rochdale. The LAA celebrated the centenary of Waugh's birth on June 23rd 1917. The LAA's magazine recorded:

Edwin Waugh

"Our glorious meeting at Waugh's Well...will long live in the memories of those who were privileged to take part in it. Despite somewhat gloomy weather, the chilly winds, and the long steep ascent, an assemblage of several hundred persons, of both sexes and all ages, gathered to pay

.[204] Edwin Waugh *Poems and Songs* Manchester 1883 p.121

eloquent and heartfelt tribute to the dead poet who had so loved and so immortalised the district."[205]

Waugh's Well, c 1890

Waugh's Well, 1985. The author and his daughters!

---

[205] *The Record*, August 1917

Two contingents set off for the top, one starting from Waterfoot, led by Samuel Compston, the other from Edenfield. By skilful organisation, the two parties arrived at Fo' Edge simultaneously. Compston read a paper before the assembled throng, commenting that *"if patriotism is a virtue, especially in these days, surely county clanship, in no narrow sense, is a virtue also."*

He continued to tell the story of the well and how it came to be a memorial to the poet. The farm was, in the mid-1860s, occupied by Bill and Ann Taylor, with the man of the house better known as 'Bill o'Johnny's'. Waugh stayed there for a while, as part of his 'drying out' regime!

A group of Waugh's friends decided to erect a stone by the well to celebrate their beloved poet, and it was dedicated to Waugh in 1866. The actual stonework as we know it today wasn't fully completed until Easter 1881 (or possibly 1882) when 'Bob o'Dick o'Giles's' from the neighbouring Slacks Farm completed the job, complete with the seating on which you can now enjoy a picnic while enjoying the superb views.

Compston ended his speech with some lines from Waugh:

> *"But oh! For the hills where the heather-cock springs*
> *From his nest in the bracken, with dew on his wings!*
> *Where the heather-flower sweetens the lone highland lea,*
> *And the mountain-winds whistle, so fresh and so free!"*

Each July there is a walk up to Fo' Edge where Waugh's poems are read, amidst the wild moorland he loved so much. In 1966, a century after the well's original dedication, members of the Lancashire Authors Association and Edwin Waugh Dialect Society helped to restore it. A bronze head of Waugh was fitted into the stone work and it was generally 'fettled'. A crowd of over 400 gathered on July 16th 1966 for the re-dedication, perhaps rivalling the numbers who assembled on that breezy cold day in 1917.[206]

It makes for a magnificent walk, whichever you approach it. On a blustery May morning two of us set off from Turn Village and walked up the old 'Coal Road' along the Rossendale Way. The last time I was there was nearly 40 years ago, so it was good to re-acquaint myself with this very special place in Lancashire's cultural heritage. The monument also commemorates Rossendale dialect poet Harry Craven and local naturalist and walker Ward Ogden.

---

[206] See 'The Centenary of a Moorland Well' by Ronald Digby in *Lancashire Authors' Anthology* ed. John P. Berry, 1984. Waugh is also commemorated in 'The Edwin Waugh' at Heywood – a Wetherspoon's pub which has some excellent displays on the poet.

Edwin Waugh's legacy is honoured and promoted by the Edwin Waugh Dialect Society, which – at least in normal times – meets regularly in Waugh's home town of Rochdale. The society organises an annual prize-giving, which is always a night to remember with music and conviviality, as well as the summer-time ramble to Waugh's Well. Here's some lines from the poet which are appropriate to Fo' Edge:

> *"Oh lay me down in moorland ground,*
> *And make it my last bed,*
> *With the heathery wilderness around,*
> *And the bonny lark o'erhead:*
> *Let fern and ling around me cling,*
> *And Green moss o'er me creep;*
> *And the sweet wild mountain breezes sing*
> *Above my slumbers deep"* [207]

Members of the Edwin Waugh Dialect Society on their annual pilgrimage.
Photo courtesy of Edwin Waugh Dialect Society

---

[207] *Poems and Songs* p.6 (second series) Oldham 1889

26. Satisfying the Soul: Allen Clarke's philosophy and spirituality

"If your religion, whatever it be, satisfies your soul and makes you a good neighbour and citizen, stick to it, but be tolerant to those of other views. Whatever you do, don't quarrel about the next world, but busy yourself trying to make this world better for everybody. I have nothing against the Bible and other creeds. They fill their place and do their work. But I think they do need the supplement of modern Spiritualism." – Allen Clarke, *Where is Heaven?*

Clarke was a deeply spiritual man. He wrote several books which directly addressed fundamental questions of existence, including *The Eternal Question - is there a life after death?, What is Man?, Where is Heaven?, This Workaday World and the Next* as well as numerous articles. His philosophy, influenced by 'theosophy', a blend of Hinduism and Buddhism aimed at a western audience, with Spiritualism and the writings of Walt Whitman, runs through *Moorlands and Memories*. Clarke found something deeply spiritual in his beloved Lancashire moors. Here he is lying in the grass, taking a break on a cycle ride back from Blackpool to Bolton, close to what he christened 'Teddy Ashton's Well' just south of Abbey Village:

"I lie on the green carpet by the crystal well, looking at the moorlands and the old farm, thinking of past and present, and musing of life and its mystery and beauty and wonder. The blue-bottle buzzing about the singing brooklet (wise insect to prefer the country to the town), the coloured butterfly flying over the grass, the horse feeding by the roadside, the two birds hopping about the moorland wall dividing two fields, the farmer's lass bringing her pail to the well, the wild roses in the lane, the white flowers on the bramble bushes, the grass that is rustling at my ear, the rushes in the brook – all these are life – they are alive in their own way, all these shapes and forms from grass to human being...are but various manifestations and degrees of the same force, produced by the sun's action upon the chemical elements of the earth, and the Divine Power at the back of it all...."

He continues his reflections: *" Is it then that the same life is on me as in the blade of grass? I wonder and wonder at the riddle. But one thing is sure. Everywhere something invisible, irresistible is ever surging, every materialising into life – the life of herb, of tree, and beast and man. The grass is just as alive as we are – I feel kinship to it – though in a different and less developed manner. I guess that even the stones on the hill, the pebbles in the brook, are alive too, in their way. Man can manufacture everything but life. He can make an aeroplane – but he cannot make a midge.*"[208]

Death and resurrection

And nothing has changed; all is well. *Moorlands and Memories* is peppered with philosophical speculations, Whitmanesque sayings, spiritual questioning. It is a deeply religious – or spiritual – book. He frequently reflects on death. He knew death well, having experienced the death of his first wife only months after their wedding. Two of his children died tragically. Within four years of publication of *Moorlands and Memories*, his second wife, Eliza, would be dead from breast cancer. In the chapter 'The Road to Simnel Town' he meditates in Tonge Cemetery, where his grandmother is buried. He urges us not to 'be dismal' about death and remember that "*the severance is but for a little while, that there is really no death. That life continues in another sphere.*"[209]

He goes on to quote the words of Walt Whitman, from 'Song of Myself':

"The dead are alive and well somewhere,
The smallest sprout shows there is really no death,
And if ever there was it led forward to life,
All goes onward, nothing collapses,
And to die is different from what any one supposed, and luckier...
Did you think life was so well provided for, and
Death, the purport of all life, is not well provided for?"[210]

By the beginnings of the 20th century Clarke had become a convinced spiritualist. The story of his 'conversion' is told in *The Eternal Question* and *This Workaday World and the Next*. His second wife, Eliza ('Lila') - who appears so frequently in *Moorlands and Memories* - was a 'natural medium'. Clarke produces evidence suggesting that she could communicate with his first wife.

Today, we easily dismiss 'spiritualism' as a cult and so much mumbo-jumbo. At the time Clarke was writing it was a very popular belief, particularly amongst educated workers in the North of England. Being a spiritualist and a socialist often went together, and Clarke typified the combination.[211]

---

208 *Moorlands* pp.155-6

209 Moorlands p.267

210 *Moorlands* p.269 and Walt Whitman *Song of Myself* part 6

211 See Logie Barrow, *Independent Spirits: Plebeian Spiritualists 1850-1910,* 1989

A walk up Old Hall Clough and spiritual awakening

Clarke's spiritual self, and its roots in the Lancashire countryside, meld together in one of the last chapters of *Moorlands Memories*, where he takes us up 'Old Hall Clough', which lies just off Chorley New Road. He sets the scene beautifully:

"On a summer afternoon, when the sun was hot, and the day was sweet, I laid my bicycle down, and reclined on the gentle grass under the shade of some oak trees on the bank of a little lake, from whose waters a cooling breeze came refreshingly. Behind me was the little glen (or clough) up which I had come, across the water was a farm within a garden, sunshiny drowsiness all over it; in a field close by, the cows were resting lazily, in front of me, in the distance, I could see the grey and purple moorland hills and the blue sky above them. "[212]

Clarke reflects on existence and the deepest of questions about our life on this earth. "*Shall we never know,*" he asks, "*the meaning of man, and why he builds houses and towns, and strives and struggles to build other things greater than towns and cities...shall we never know why he has evolved from ape-like ancestor, with no thought and no invention, into the creature that today thinks about everything, and devises the most amazing machines and structures...making hold cathedrals and infernal cannons out of the same substance. Shall we never know the beginning and the meaning of man?*"[213]

Old Hall Clough, much as Clarke would have seen it

[212] *Moorlands* p.323

[213] *Moorlands* p.325

Clarke takes us through a catalogue of unanswered questions around death, love, poetry, philosophy, 'all the things that build the body and make the mind of the man.' As he meditated by the lake, the answer, as he describes it, came 'from within' and from the surrounding environment – the grass, trees, water and surrounding hills and wildlife. It's a deep, evolutionary vision based around humanity's growth towards maturity. It's a sensory development in which we progress from 'slime to soul', " *developing first a sense to feel things, then senses to see and hear things, followed by senses that opened to him knowledge of the form and colour and music of the phenomena of the universe; every development unfolding more and more of the secrets of being...*" [214]

In his 'answer' humanity's evolution is measured in millennia, a slow evolution towards solving the problems that have been wrestled with over the centuries: the meaning of life and death, affection and separation, memory and mourning. For, he says, "*the process and purpose of evolution is the divine development from grub unto God. From grub to God is the tale of man; and all is well.*"[215]

Amongst the blossoms and butterflies

Allen Clarke's spiritual thoughts are further developed in his other, directly philosophical, works. But it is in the earth, 'amongst the blossoms and butterflies' where Clarke finds his inspiration. You can still find it. It hasn't vanished these last 100 years. Walk or cycle (you need good tyres) up Old Hall Clough from Chorley New Road and you will find that same pool, with the former farm, now a home but still called 'Old Hall Farm', across the water. Stop and reflect by the stone seat, facing the pool, erected in 1987 to honour the memory of a young lad called Sam Roberts who died in a tragic road accident.

Then, continue onto High Rid Lane, turning left along this ancient and rather bumpy road by the picturesque High Rid Reservoir. Turn right when you get to the former High Rid Farm and go along the lane towards Higher Wilson Fold Farm where you'll find an old settlement of houses: a classic Lancashire fold, or 'fowt'.

If you take a right and continue up the public footpath towards The Blundell Arms (originally The Moorgate Inn) look out for a wooded glade to your right, at the start of the path. You will see the grave of Jennifer Nuttall-Wolf, an accomplished violinist and lover of these moors, who passed on in May 2020. She is buried, like Roger Worthington on Holcombe Moor, in a small grave of her own. The ceremony on June 4th 2020 was conducted by Unitarian minister and Whitman lover, Tony McNeile.

Everything connects, and all is well.

---

[214] *Moorlands* p.326

[215] *Moorlands* p.327

27. Towards the Co-operative Commonwealth

"I still cherish the vision, and I still hold the faith, that in spite of everything against it, humanity is evolving towards the ideal commonwealth"[216]

Allen Clarke's political and social views were consistent throughout his life, though his affiliations changed. I'd describe him as a libertarian socialist. He joined the Marxist-inclined Social Democratic Federation in the late 1880s and then seems to have switched allegiance to the Independent Labour Party. As we have already seen, he was actively involved in the non-partisan Labour Church. Quite a big part of him leant towards anarchism, of the non-violent Tolstoyan sort. The great Russian thinker was one of Clarke's biggest influences and the two corresponded.

Clarke's idea of socialism was summed up in the idea of 'the co-operative commonwealth' which was a society based on Kropotkin's idea of mutual aid and small-scale production, not centralised state ownership which socialism came to be synonymous with.

The idea of a 'co-operative commonwealth' had a powerful attraction throughout much of the first half of the 20th century. It was central to the 'ethical socialism' which put down deep roots in the North before the First World War. The creation of the post-Empire 'Commonwealth' was perhaps an attempt by some Labour politicians with roots stretching back to the early days of the socialist movement to create something that everyone could be proud of. To me, it has a far more attractive resonance than the much-abused and misunderstood term that 'socialism' has become today.

Clarke embraced the spirit of co-operation. He saw the co-operative movement, which became so powerful a force in the North, as being about much more than the 'divi'. It was about a different way of life, contrasting with selfish individualism. In one of his most interesting books, *The Eternal Question*, he advises:

"...as regards politics, all government by physical force is wrong, and that as regards work and wages and affairs of livelihood, the only true order is co-operation – communistic co-operation - every man to do what he can and to have what he needs; amassing of individual fortunes being utterly unrighteous." [217]

The Daisy Colony scheme and Tolstoy

Clarke did his best to put principles into practice. Between 1903 and 1906 he

---

[216] Allen Clarke, *Liverpool Weekly Post*, March 23rd 1935

[217] *The Eternal Question – is there another life?* 1919 ed. p.220

attempted to create a 'co-operative community' near Blackpool – 'The Daisy Colony'. He and a few others rented some land at Carleton and started to grow produce, with the aim of becoming self-sustaining.

It was very much inspired by Tolstoyan principles and Clarke sent copies of his 'Daisy Colony' articles in *The Northern Weekly* (above) to Tolstoy who responded by wishing his venture every success. [218]

Tolstoy wrote:

"Dear friend Allen Clarke, I was glad to have news from you. I wish success to your scheme (Daisy Colony – ed.). It is the beginning of a very great and wonderful work which will have to be done sooner or later. Your book, 'The Effects of the Factory System', translated into Russian is very much appreciated. Now I will try to translate one of your novels. I have not read them yet, but judging by the opinion of the press, and my own based on the book I know, they must have the same merits as The Effects of the Factory System.

Your friend, Leo Tolstoy"

Sadly, even the backing of the great man proved insufficient and – like so many similar ventures at the time – it fell apart. However, it seems that *Effects of the Factory System* was translated into Russian, though I've never been able to trace a copy.

CENTRAL PREMISES,
Comprising Grocery, Confectionery, Jewellery, Furniture, and Boot and Shoe Departments.

The main Bolton Co-operative Society store, on Bridge Street c. 1908

---

[218] See *Lancashire's Romantic Radical* p.48

The experience did not diminish his faith in co-operative principles. He admired the 'Rochdale Pioneers' and wrote a novel about them, published by the CWS in Manchester. *The Men Who Fought For Us* shows Clarke at his best, weaving a story of working class life and 'gradely' men and women striving to achieve great things for their community. In the novel, the handful of former Chartists and Owenites establish their little shop on Toad Lane in Rochdale. After many trials and tribulations it starts to grow.

In true Allen Clarke style there is a happy ending in terms of both romance and the success of the co-operative movement. It is Christmas, 1843 and he muses, *"...something had begun. Common-sense Co-operation, child of Communist Vision, united to Workaday Business, was on its feet, starting to walk. The bantling, so long and so assiduously nursed and tended by the twenty-eight pioneers of Rochdale, was standing up and toddling about."*[219]

Co-operation in Bolton

Perhaps Clarke was a bit disappointed that the co-operative movement was established in Rochdale rather than Bolton. In *Moorlands and Memories* he tells us about the beginnings of co-operation in his home town. He describes a stroll up Derby Street and St Helen's Road, where he passes 'The Half-way House' pub.

"It is an historic inn, at least to Co-operators, for in this old tavern the Bolton Co-operative Movement had its start. There had been a previous attempt to run a co-operative Stores in Bolton in 1851, but it was not until 1859 that Co-operation was successfully launched in Bolton, and a woman began it – Mrs 'Gladdy' Ashton, landlady of the Half-Way House."[220]

'Gladdy' – or Mary Ann Ashton - offered a small shop next door to the pub, at 37a Derby Street, to a group of "*Bolton Moor weavers, mostly Chartists*" who included John Kirkman, William Crankshaw and John Morton. The shop began trading on November 5th 1859 and it grew steadily before opening larger premises on Bridge Street in 1867.[221] Mrs Ashton was the first treasurer of the society, a worthy predecessor of Sarah Reddish of Bolton who became a national figure in the Co-operative Movement and president of the Women's Co-operative Guild. Clarke described her as *"a socialist lady speaker who has done a deal of useful work, both on the platform and off."*[222]

---

[219] *The Men Who Fought For Us,* Manchester 1914, p.273

[220] *Moorlands* p.307

[221] See also F.W. Peaples *History of Great and Little Bolton Co-operative Society*, Bolton 1909

[222] 'Ben Adhem' (Allen Clarke) 'Amongst the Agitators' *Teddy Ashton's Northern Weekly* September 30th 1905

Clarke, being the idealist that he was, was never really content with the 'Co-op's' focus on retail activities. He saw much of the co-operative movement of his day being the 'retail' equivalent of trades-unionism: self-protection but certainly not about ushering in 'the co-operative commonwealth'. Yet Clarke admits that co-operation achieved much though being able to make wholesome, unadulterated food available at a price working people could afford.

Perhaps the success of the co-operative movement in its early years, which it has sadly lost, was the strong degree of local ownership. As well as the Bolton society, there was a powerful co-operative society serving Farnworth and Kearsley with a large store on Market Street. There was a photograph in the store of my great-grandfather, Tom Molyneaux, when he was captain of the Moses Gate Cycling Club, which may well have been affiliated to the Co-op movement. The framed photo, which my gran always pointed out, disappeared when the store was demolished in 1971. The society had merged into the Bolton and Wigan society the previous year.

Co-operation in Bolton today is represented by the national 'Co-op' - the Co-operative Group. It became 'Bolton and District Co-operative Society' in 1963 and then part of 'Bolton and Wigan Co-operative Society in 1970. Further mergers occurred until it became part of the Co-operative Group.

Small individual co-operative enterprises have ebbed and flowed. Most recently, 'The Kitchen' – a workers' co-operative cafe and shop on Great Moor Street - closed its doors in early 2020. Yet the surge in the number of 'credit unions' is an example of 'financial' co-operation at work. The idea of co-operation and mutual aid is very much alive, as witnessed during the coronavirus and the upsurge of initiatives calling themselves 'mutual aid' groups. Kropotkin would have been delighted! And so, I'm sure, would Allen Clarke.

Perhaps we really are still evolving towards that ideal commonwealth. Could we apply that ideal to a revived Lancashire region?

28. Visions of a new Lancashire

"I would like to see Lancashire a cluster of small villages and towns, each fixed solid on its own agricultural base, doing its own spinning and weaving; with its theatre, gymnasium, schools, libraries, baths and all things necessary for body and soul. Supposing the energy, time and talent that have been given to manufacture and manufacturing inventions had been given to agriculture and agricultural inventions, would not there have been as wonderful results in food production as there have been in cotton goods production?" [223]

That was Clarke writing in 1895. Utopian? Perhaps slightly (we need our utopian visions!) but there's an element of realism there too. He recognised that capitalism had unleashed enormously powerful productive forces, but not necessarily with the best results. What Clarke was saying over a century ago is being said by many green activists and thinkers today and what Gandhi preached in his own time. Humanity has the resources and skills to create a better world, for everyone; the consequences of not trying are worsening climate change and all that follows from it.

Clarke looked forward to a Lancashire that was a greener, more self-sufficient place – within a co-operative rather than a capitalist system. Now, as we emerge from the coronavirus pandemic, is the ideal time to think differently about the world we live in.

Vision and hope

The Lancashire of Allen Clarke's day has changed in so many ways, though the moorlands he describes remain largely unchanged. In the towns, gone are the mill chimneys with their attendant pollution and poor working conditions inside the factory walls. But we have also lost some of the civic pride and buoyancy of the great Lancashire boroughs including Clarke's beloved Bolton.

His prophecy, in *Effects of the Factory System*, that the cotton industry was doomed has finally come to be. Most of the mills that you could once see from the top of Smithills Dean Road, described so vividly in *Moorlands and Memories*, have been demolished. A few have survived but many are in poor condition, with only the prospect of demolition ahead of them unless something is done.

Lancashire has yet to find a new role that can build on its past achievements, without just becoming a dull collection of retail parks, charity shops and sprawling suburbia, nor indeed a heritage theme park. Most of the surviving Lancashire

---

[223] *Effects of the Factory System*, p.174

mills, perhaps with the exception of Manchester's Ancoats, don't have the wonderful mix of creative industries, office space and living accommodation that has been achieved with some of the mills in Yorkshire. At Saltaire, Salt's Mill is perhaps the finest example, though rivalled by the Dean Clough Mills in Halifax. More should be done to protect our Lancashire mills and find good uses for them. Why should Yorkshire have all the fun?

Allen Clarke would have loved the idea of putting the mill buildings to better use - as places to live, but also as office and art space, recreational centres and performance areas. How about mill roof gardens? There'd be no shortage of space, with room to grow fruit and veg. Time for the 'Incredible Edible Mill'!

We also need to build new, inspirational buildings that can take their place alongside the fine architecture bequeathed us by past generations. We need a vision, at least as radical as that of T.H. Mawson, of what our towns and cities should look like in the next 20 years, not what developers think is 'good enough' for us and makes the quickest return for them.

Looking down to Bolton from above Smithills. A few mills survive, minus chimneys

Sharing the same skies: the moors for everyone

Alongside a vibrant urban society, economy and culture, we need to make the best of our countryside, the 'green lungs' that make Lancashire so special.

The events of 1896, when thousands of Bolton people fought to protect their countryside from the encroachments of landlords, demonstrated that people's love of their countryside isn't new, nor an exclusively middle-class preserve.

The countryside has stronger legal protection than it had in Clarke's day, notably through post-war legislation passed by Labour. But we need to be vigilant. Recent suggestions to strengthen the law of trespass could potentially be used to criminalise what is currently a civil offence. The Ramblers are mounting a strong campaign to have the ideas abandoned. Possible changes to planning law could affect places on the fringes of the countryside, not currently protected.

Perhaps the biggest immediate threat to countryside access is a combination of some landowners' deliberate policy of discouraging access, combined with lack of a strong local voice for walkers. Whilst writing this book I found several examples of old footpaths, clearly marked as rights of way, that had fallen into disuse and effectively become impassable. Signage had been removed. In some cases landowners were using the 'coronavirus' situation to illegally close off public rights of way. It's not all one-way. Some landowners, large and small, behave responsibly and encourage access to the countryside; it's fair enough to expect all visitors to behave responsibly.

Access for all means better public transport and car-free countryside

Another threat is the private car. When Clarke was writing the roads he cycled along were – if admittedly a bit bumpy – quiet and devoid of traffic at weekends. How that has changed. Places like Rivington, Pendle and Holcombe can be heaving with cars and motor bikes at weekends. At the same time, many stations that gave walkers access to the countryside, have closed. Stations that Clarke used and wrote about - Chatburn in the Ribble Valley, Garstang and its light railway to Knott End, Helmshore, Waterfoot and Turton and Edgworth have gone. They should come back. Scores of bus services that once gave access to surrounding villages have either disappeared or are so infrequent to be unusable.

Never mind HS2, let's rebuild a world-class local transport network. For a fraction of the cost of that high-speed white elephant, we could have a network of modern, zero-emission trams and buses serving town and country, feeding in to a core rail network.

Modern cycling: a small team, with friend, head up towards Winter Hill, July 2020

One of the few bright spots during the coronavirus outbreak has been the remarkable growth in cycling. Clarke and his friends Johnston and Wild would be delighted. Quiet roads, good weather and time on your hands was the ideal combination. Cycle shops have enjoyed a boon. I hope this renewed interest in cycling will survive, particularly if the Government puts its money where its mouth is and provides funding to expand cycle facilities in both town and country.

People will still use their car to get out into the countryside and that needs to be managed and provided for. Car parks can be ugly, but so can cars parked alongside verges. The more alternatives there are available, the less likely we are to assume that the only way to enjoy the countryside is by that form of transport which does most to disfigure it. In 1907, Clarke used one of his characters in *The Red Flag* to describe cars as 'fume-pots on wheels'. How right he was!

Why not copy the example of some of the national parks in the United States, which prohibit car access to the most sensitive areas? If you get there by car, leave it in a 'parking lot' and either walk, get on a local bus or hire a bike. It could work in some of our national parks and popular visitor locations such as Rivington. The exciting plans for a 'South Pennines' regional park could include sensitive measures to restrict visitors' car access and promote use of public transport, cycling and walking.

A few months ago I might have been sceptical at the possibility of moving away from a car-based culture. After three months of the lockdown and the huge upsurge in cycling and walking, perhaps there is cause for hope.

Is Lancashire worth preserving?

It's not just the mills, nor even the moors. It's about what kind of Lancashire we want to live in.

Allen Clarke's Lancashire has been shrunk by an undemocratic diktat in the 1970s. Nobody asked the people of Bolton, Rochdale, Oldham, Wigan and other towns if they wanted to be part of 'Greater Manchester'. We have an elected mayor but without the democratic oversight of an elected council – which at least the original 'Greater Manchester' Council had, before it was abolished by Mrs Thatcher in 1986. Something else we weren't asked about.

Allen Clarke was a strong believer in municipal reform and backed Solomon Partington's Municipal Reform League. There's a need for something like that but on a bigger scale, addressing the huge democratic deficit in the English regions as well as the loss of power by local government. Samuel Compston spoke of the virtue of 'county clanship, in no narrow sense'. He was on to something and his wording was carefully chosen. Regional pride does not pre-suppose antipathy to other regions and nations, and it needs to include everyone *within* the region. But it requires a democratic voice, not just one person elected every few years as 'mayor', nor a collection of local authority leaders whose prime loyalty is to their own council ward.

Yorkshire has been quicker off the mark and the Campaign for a Yorkshire Parliament has won wide cross-party support; the Yorkshire Party has made several local gains. The Yorkshire-based 'Same Skies Collective' has developed some fresh new ways of thinking about regionalism.

Here, there's a Friends of Real Lancashire but the issue needs a higher profile and cross-party support. A reformed Lancashire that includes Greater Manchester and Merseyside makes sense as an economic unit but also chimes with people's identities – in a way that artificial 'city regions' never will. 'Greater Manchester' has reduced the once proudly-independent county boroughs to the status of satellites - commuter suburbs of Manchester (or 'Manctopia' as it was described in an excellent TV programme recently).

Nearly 50 years on from the creation of 'Greater Manchester' our 'city region' still has precious little legitimacy and if there was a referendum tomorrow on being part of Lancashire or 'Greater Manchester' I have little doubt about the result.

Regional democracy is the next big jump for our political system with regional assemblies, elected proportionately, taking real powers out of Westminster, backed up by strong well-resourced local government which has the right scale (not too big!). That means medium-sized towns, such as Darwen, Heywood, Farnworth, Radcliffe and others, having their own voice and powers, co-operating with their neighbouring communities on issues of mutual concern within a Lancashire 'co-operative commonwealth'.

That co-operation should extend further, across the North. Why not a 'Northern Federation' of regions – Lancashire, Yorkshire, the North-East and Cumbria, collaborating on issues of joint concern, such as strategic transport links and academic co-operation? As the late Jo Cox (a committed regionalist) said, "we have far more in common than what divides us."

A Red Rose Co-operative Commonwealth?

Good, democratic governance must be about addressing inequality, jobs, the environment, health, education and having a thriving and diverse cultural sector. Allen Clarke's vision in 1895, of locally-based and socially-owned units of production make sense in a modern digital age, co-operating as equals with partners across the globe.

His idea of a 'co-operative commonwealth' could certainly work at a Lancashire level; after all, it's where co-operation began. Allen Clarke, with Solomon Partington, Sarah Reddish and Samuel Compston looking over his shoulder, would have said "what are you waiting for?"

And we can't wait. The coronavirus pandemic has focused people's minds on the dysfunctional way we have lived our lives. An even bigger threat is climate change which requires re-thinking every aspect of how we live, travel, work and play.

Now is the time to create that Allen Clarke's vision of a 'Lancashire Co-operative Commonwealth' that can, in the words of Clarke's heroine, Rose Hilton – get agate with the job of *"washing the smoky dust off the petals of the red rose."*

Beneath the red rose: community and culture at The Barlow, Edgworth

Last word

Let Allen Clarke, and myself, have the last word...

> *"We trust you have enjoyed these rambles and reflections as much as we have, and we hope you will repeat them again and again, in the flesh as well as in the print, finding in our moorlands and their memories health for the body, happiness for the heart, and vision for the soul."* [224]

Vision for the soul: Looking across to Rivington Pike and the Irish Sea from The Two Lads

[224] *Moorlands* p.341, with slight amendments

Further reading

Books by Allen Clarke – out of print but obtainable (with luck)

Moorlands and Memories, (1920, 1924, 1986)

Effects of the Factory System (1899, 1986)

Windmill Land (1916, 1986)

Other books by the author

Lancashire's Romantic Radical – the life and writings of Allen Clarke/Teddy Ashton (author, 2009)

With Walt Whitman in Bolton: Spirituality, Sex and Socialism in a Northern Mill Town, 3rd edition (author, 2019)

Socialism with a Northern Accent (Lawrence and Wishart 2012)

Will Yo' Come O' Sunday Mornin'? The Winter Hill Trespass of 1896, 2nd ed. 1996

Other publications

The publications of our local history societies are immensely useful. See the websites of Halliwell Local History Society, Horwich Heritage and Turton Local History Society

Winter Hill and Anglezarke Scrapbook by Dave Lane, Derek Cartwright and Garry Rhodes (2019) is a mine of information

Lancashire Loominary

Lancashire Loominary is the publishing business of Paul Salveson. The name is a tribute to J.T. Staton's *Lankishire Loominary* which he edited in the 1850s and 1860s (with several variations on the title). Most of the work I publish is my own writing. My occasional newsletter, *The Northern Weekly Salvo*, can be read or downloaded at www.paulsalveson.org.uk

For full details of my books visit www.lancashireloominary.co.uk

Available

The Works: My first novel, set in Horwich Loco Works in the 1970s and 1980s: life, love and politics in a time of strife. Paperback £12.99

With Walt Whitman in Bolton: spirituality, sex and socialism in a Northern Mill Town – 3rd ed. 2019. The remarkable story of Lancashire's links with the great American poet. Fully illustrated. Paperback £9.90

Lancashire's Romantic Radical – the life and writings of Allen Clarke/Teddy Ashton - 2009. A well illustrated account of Clarke's life and his writings, both fiction and non-fiction. Paperback (large format) £10

How to order

Details and order form are on wwwlancashireloominary.co.uk

Books can be ordered through Amazon - and *The Works* is available on kindle at £4.99.

You can order direct from the author, please add on £3.00 for postage and make cheques to 'Paul Salveson'. Send to 109 Harpers Lane, Bolton BL1 6HU. You can also pay by bank transfer to my account: Dr P S Salveson sort code 53-61-07 account 23448954. Email me at paul.salveson@myphone.coop to let me know, with your address.

The £3.00 postage charge applies to orders for more than one book i.e. if you order a copy of both *The Works* and *Walt Whitman* you just pay £3.00 to cover the full order. This only applies to the UK. Please enquire if you are in foreign parts.

If you live within 5 miles of Bolton I can do free delivery, by bike. Allow a few days in case the weather is bad.

Events and Talks

I'm available to give talks to groups about aspects of my work. Please email me on paul.salveson@myphone.coop or ring 07795 008691. Charges vary depending on the group – if you're a small voluntary group with limited funds, it's usually free. Otherwise there's a small fee.

What readers said of *The Works*

"I picked it up the other day and read it in two days which is something I rarely do. It usually takes me weeks to complete a book (my wife always complains it takes her about three days). Maybe it was because of my railway connection but I think not , it was a good story with characters I recognised It captured the era and what was going on , not much has changed has it ! But it had a real 'Lancashire' feel about it." – Peter, Preston

"I thoroughly enjoyed reading *The Works*, the mixture of facts and fiction all combined to tell a good story of what might have been. Previously I only knew the basics about Horwich so the history of the town and the works, inseparable, was something of a revelation to me. The characters carried the story along well and for me some of them - like Midge - were very convincing." - George, Littleborough

"I enjoyed reading *The Works*. It is a warm-hearted (and counter factual!) tale of how the world-famous Horwich Loco Work is saved from British Rail Engineering's attempted closure by a workers' cooperative drawing inspiration from the Upper Clyde Shipbuilders. I enjoyed the descriptions of the local politics and trade union life of the 1970s and '80s before and during the Thatcher years." – Mike, Sheffield

"Thank you so much for delivering your book. This was for a gift and received nothing but amazing comments on the book and the pictures and the social history for our town." – Ashleigh, Farnworth

" I loved *The Works*, a novel full of vivid and warm Lancashire characters with a truly interesting plotline that piqued my interest in the social and political landscape of the time. I was sad to see the last line of the book, hurry up Paul Salveson and write another!" – Amanda, Horwich

Special Bi-Centennial edition 2019

With Walt Whitman in Bolton

Spirituality, Sex and Socialism in a Northern Mill Town

Paul Salveson

Lancashire's Romantic Radical

The life and writings of Allen Clarke/Teddy Ashton

Paul Salveson

Little Northern Books

£15.00